Price To Value

Intelligent Speculation Using

The Decision Filters of Munger and Buffett

By Bud Labitan

Copyright © 2010

ISBN 978-0-557-36041-3

"Why should that apple always descend perpendicularly to the ground. Why should it not go sideways, or upwards? But constantly to the earth's centre? Assuredly, the reason is, that the earth draws it. There must be a drawing power in matter."

Sir Isaac Newton

TABLE OF CONTENTS

ACKNOWLEDGMENTS

This book is dedicated with Love to my daughter Victoria Labitan and the graduating class of 2010. It is intended to enhance all readers' decision making skills.

I am grateful to my family and friends for their support in the writing of this manuscript. Thanks to Janine Rueth, Frank Betz, Paul Lountzis, Joe Koster, James Altucher, Ron McColly, Tony Taleff, Herb Rueth, Rosemary Rueth, Brett Baker, Clark Labitan, Chuck Labitan, Dirk Suter, Dr. Karl Schwartz, and Dr. Chin Pham for their reading, samples, and critique. Some of the quotations in this book were approved for use in the "Four Filters Invention" book. This does not imply any endorsement of either book.

Bud Labitan

budlabitan@aol.com

INTRODUCTION

"Price To Value" is about Intelligent Speculation. It's about using the amazing "Decision Filters" of Charlie Munger and Warren Buffett. These framing filters offer us the opportunity to enhance our decision framing and decision making skills in both investing and speculation. This book is intended to inspire clearer thinking by suggesting a better approach to structuring a decision. An improved approach to thinking rationally can take our skills from good to better.

How can we use this framework to improve our speculative decision making? We can use it to help us separate fact from fiction. Readers will benefit from this material if it stimulates better thinking into the most important factors crucial to decision making.

Readers new to this material should first know that Buffett and Munger are the chairman and vice-chairman of Berkshire Hathaway Inc. Benjamin Graham was Warren Buffett's teacher at Columbia University, and the author of *The Intelligent Investor* and *Security Analysis*. Many good books have been written about all three men. Their investing and speculation methods have credibility because they have produced consistently profitable results over a long period of time.

The decision framing model discussed in this book can be applied across different asset classes. First, this book presents the four investing decision filters in simplified terms. Then, it extends these ideas by looking into the intelligent speculation ideal described by Benjamin Graham in his tenth lecture of 1946. In that lecture, he repeated his definition for "speculation." The distinction between investment and speculation is this: "An investment operation is one which, on thorough analysis, promises safety of principal and a satisfactory return. Operations not meeting these requirements are speculative." In either operation, speculation or investment, Charlie Munger's statement is useful: "You have to understand the odds and have the discipline to bet only when the odds are in your favor."[1]

Benjamin Graham suggested that the intelligent participant in Wall Street would try to follow the technique of the bookmaker rather than the technique of the man who bets on the horses. Since much of Wall Street activity must have elements of chance in it, Graham said that "the sound idea would be to measure these chances as accurately as you can, and play the game in the direction of having the odds on your side."

According to Graham, "Intelligent speculation presupposes at least that the mathematical possibilities are not against the speculation, basing the measurement of these odds on experience and the careful weighing of relevant facts.[2]" Since the decision filters weigh the relevant facts necessary for business success, I wondered if the same process could be applied to framing an intelligent business speculation. Can the addition and subtraction of qualitative factors raise the odds for speculative success?

In my book, "The Four Filters Invention of Warren Buffett and Charlie Munger," I wrote about their rational four filters investing **decision framing process**. This process has worked as an effective set of mental tools. The Four Filters are a search for: "1. Understandable first-class businesses, with 2. enduring competitive advantages, accompanied by 3. first-class management, available at 4. a bargain price."[3] In my view, they invented an investing process that is underappreciated by the business and academic communities. Their filters help us frame our investing process correctly, and they help us prevent foolish and costly investing losses. Using this process, we become better investors by improving the way we think about businesses and "intelligent decision framing."

As readers may remember, this innovative process uses the most important factors necessary to frame the decision. It raised their odds of investing success because the process contained all the important factors needed for business success. These four decision groups include products, enduring customers, managers, and margin-of-safety... all in one mixed "qualitative + quantitative" decision process.

Imagine combining four or five decision groups of important facts together in order to make a better structured speculation. In both investing and speculation, the ideal strategy is to minimize irrelevant and distracting factors. Acquiring this ability can raise your attitude and thinking effectiveness. As we consider productive and unproductive factors, we can imagine that theoretically fuzzy area where correlation and causality begin to converge. However, let us explore real factors that influence both value and price.What about the filter factors effects on intelligent speculation? First, think of how they developed a better understanding of a business and its products? Charlie Munger said, "We read a lot. I don't know anyone who's wise who doesn't read a lot. But that's not enough: You have to have a temperament to grab ideas and do sensible things."[4]

Intelligent and Unintelligent Speculation

While reading through Benjamin Graham's 1946 lectures, I came across a very interesting topic in his final talk that semester. Said Graham, "there is a real difference between intelligent and unintelligent speculation, and that the methods of security analysis may often be of value in distinguishing between the two kinds of speculation. [5]" Many of these methods are still relevant and useful today.

Unintelligent Speculation

An Excerpt from
Benjamin Graham's "The Intelligent Investor"

There is intelligent speculation as there is intelligent investing. But there are many ways in which speculation may be unintelligent. Of these the foremost are:

(1) speculating when you think you are investing;

(2) speculating seriously instead of as a pastime, when you lack proper knowledge and skill for it; and

(3) risking more money in speculation than you can afford to lose.

From Ben Graham's "The Intelligent Investor." CHAPTER 1. *Investment versus Speculation: Results to Be Expected by the Intelligent Investor*

Decision Model

Since this filtration method works for investment, can they be applied to increase the probability of a successful intelligent speculation? The filter groups can be used to define positive and negative characteristics of a business or speculative situation. I think this was Graham's intent in that last talk. Ben Graham compared companies for his students. He illustrated to them the mathematical advantage of a company carrying less debt in comparison to one burdened by heavy debt obligations.

Notice the checklist nature of the investment decision filters. They serve as a logical and sensible justification mechanism. Like pilots who use a checklist prior to flying, the filters checklist helps us frame a more rational investment decision. For those of you who like a visual model of these ideas, take a look at the following diagram. It is one way to categorize and frame our thoughts about "intelligent speculation" into five decision groups.

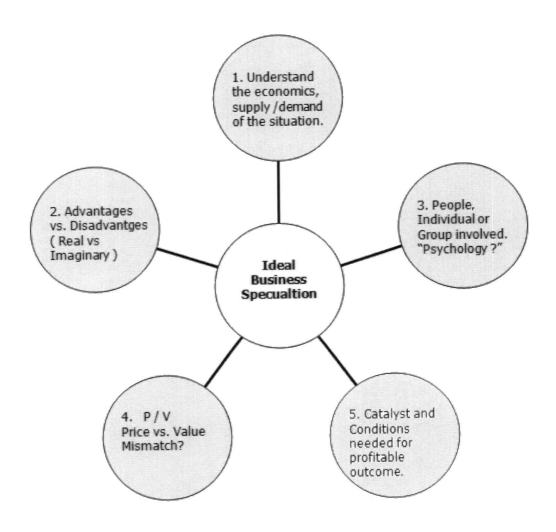

Graham-Buffett-Munger based Intelligent Speculation Model
Can this framing approach yield better odds for speculation success?
This book "Price To Value" explores these decision framing ideas.

CHAPTER ONE
UNDERSTANDING DECISION FRAMING

While writing about the four filters innovation of Buffett and Munger, I started to realize that this is an effective way to frame our important decisions. This framing process showed me the importance of including the most important factors while excluding lesser factors.

Readers may remember that Investing Filter Number One is to Develop an (Economic) Understanding of a Business and its Products. In developing an economic understanding of a business and its products, Warren Buffett framed the mental process this way: "If I were looking at a company, I would put myself in the frame of mind that I had just inherited that company, and it was the only asset my family was ever going to own. What would I do with it? What am I thinking about? What am I worried about? Who are my customers? Go out and talk to them. Find out the strengths and weaknesses of this particular company versus other ones."[6] This is the behavioral process of elaboration. It is the bit of mental work that helps us frame and develop a clearer mental picture of reality. Setting up a sensible framework of factors to include and exclude, as in filtering out things, helps to focus our investing plan.

Decision Group as a Checklist Item

Can we use a checklist for smarter and intelligent speculation? Can we develop a speculation checklist that includes the most important factors like business economics, short term competitive advantage, able people, mispricing, and other catalysts? Recall that Charlie Munger believes in using checklist routines to help us avoid a lot of errors. These errors occur because our human brains are wired to find shortcuts, or what Munger calls "shortcut types of approximations." In 1995, Charlie Munger presented a speech on the psychology of human misjudgment. In that speech, he said: "The main antidotes to miscues from Availability-Misweighing Tendency often involve procedures, including the use of checklists, which are almost always helpful."[7] This is like picking a business that is well known and admired versus picking a business that is not as well known. Our brains tend to overlook the things that are not readily in front of us. These days, psychologists call this the Availability heuristic; estimating what is more likely by what is more available in memory, which is biased toward vivid, unusual, or emotionally charged examples.

Avoid Biases

We should also avoid cognitive biases, overconfidence and irrationality. They are not helpful. A long list of thinking biases are included in the appendix of this book. Biases like stereotyping, anchoring, and attentional bias can force our thinking off track into making mistakes. Thus, the filter groups are helpful because they enforce a rational decision framing procedure. This increases the probability of investment success. Perhaps, this framing process can also increase the probability for speculative success. Remember that the filters are a search for: "Understandable first-class businesses, with enduring competitive advantages, accompanied by first-class management, available at a bargain price."[8]

Better Targeting

Recall Warren Buffett's baseball analogy: "I put heavy weight on certainty. Use probability in your favor and avoid risk. It's not risky to buy securities at a fraction of what they are worth. Don't gamble. You're dealing with a lot of silly people in the marketplace; it's like a great big casino, and everyone else is boozing. Watch for unusual circumstances. Great investment opportunities come around when excellent companies are surrounded by unusual circumstances that cause the stock to be misappraised. In appraising the odds, Ted Williams explained how he increased his probability of hitting: "To be a good hitter, you've got to get a good ball to hit. It's the first rule in the book." That good ball to hit would be the wonderful business, not the ever changing macro market. Charlie Munger said that they started thinking more about better businesses. Munger described their system this way: "We came to this notion of finding a mispriced bet and loading up when we were very confident that we were right. So we're way less diversified. And I think our system is miles better."[9]

Berkshire Hathaway (NYSE: BRKA and NYSE: BRKB) is a conglomerate holding company headquartered in Omaha, Nebraska, USA. The company averaged an annual growth in book value of 20.3% for the last 44 years, while employing large amounts of capital, and minimal debt. Their goal at Berkshire Hathaway is to maximize the average annual rate of gain in intrinsic business value on a per-share basis. Buffett and Munger have occasionally participated in special speculative situations. In his 1961 partnership letter, Warren Buffett described the kind of special situation that he was willing to speculate: "Our bread-and-butter business is buying undervalued securities and selling when-the undervaluation is corrected along with investment in "special situations" where the profit is dependent on corporate rather than market action."[10]

Focus

That dependence on business rather than market action forced the focus of prediction on the set with less number of variables. More recently, experience and conservatism guide their decisions. The lack of precise data should always urge us to use caution. In reference to reinsuring against hurricanes and earthquakes, Buffett said, "the best we can do at Berkshire is to estimate a range of probabilities for such events."[11]

Prediction and Probability

While able insurers have been fair predictors of loss, and loss reserving, how do they do it? Insurers generally use actuarial methods and models that combine past experience with future estimation. The basic idea in estimating "developed losses" is to add what has been actually paid out in the past to what they expect to pay out if the "expected loss ratio" is correct.[12] Past payouts, called losses, are presented in a table called a run-off triangle. The entries in a run-off triangle for payouts are the accumulated amounts paid out over the years for events that occurred in the specific past years of interest.

In building a better model for the intelligent framing of a speculative decision, what can we learn from these insurers? First, notice that using past data and combining it with newer predictive data is similar to Bayesian Probability. Named after Thomas Bayes, Bayesian

Probability specifies some prior probability, which is then updated with new relevant data. It has a set of procedures and a formula for performing such predictive calculations.

Causal Factors

Instead of studying correlated events, causality is the relationship between a causing event and an effect event, where the second event is a consequence of the first. The best models of study in causality are in physics and engineering. Some of you will remember from physics that force equals mass times acceleration. And, the first four chapters suggest framing methods of adding diagnostic "mass" to our speculation model. The fifth chapter will discuss catalysts and conditions, the acceleration portion of F=MA. This will not be a strict definition of acceleration. Think of it more here as a general idea about movement, and what moves an intelligent speculation. Generally, there are factors, conditions, and forces that come into play.

Our Speculation Model

Going forward, I refer to our theoretical and idealized "intelligent speculation set of factors" as our business "speculation model." Then, our ideal speculation model aims for accuracy closer to studies in causality. In the past, others have focused their studies in event correlations.[13] Here, focus on cause and effect. Think of real and potential forces that can influence both gains and losses. Having this higher idealized goal, we can think of it as Graham called it, "following the technique of the bookmaker rather than the technique of the man who bets on the horses." It involves framing our speculation model with the important "decision framing factors" and discarding the wood of unimportant decision factors.

Investment Decision Framing

Buffett and Munger frame their investment decisions by using the filters this way: "We look for understandable first-class businesses, with enduring competitive advantages, accompanied by first-class management, available at a bargain price." Play with the four filter criteria and twist them into 4 business decision groups: 1. Product Economics 2. Customers 3. Management 4. Margin of Safety. After many hours of thought and play, I concluded that the Four Filters are a remarkable intellectual achievement. They effectively combine the use of qualitative and quantitative factors. Using inversion to find 1 out of 1,000, the filters help us eliminate the lesser 999 prospects.

As our thinking progresses, how do we develop a better frame of reference? How do we increase the probability of speculation and investing success? An increasing body of literature on decision "framing" supports a tendency for people to take more risks when seeking to avoid losses as opposed to securing gains. In 1992, Takemura[14] showed that the effects of framing are likely to be lower when subjects are warned in advance that they will be required to justify their choices. Takemura also showed that the effects of framing are lessened when more time is allowed for making choices.

In trying to understand a business, remember that Buffett and Munger practice rational decision framing. In business school they call it SWOT analysis; looking for the Strengths, Weaknesses, Opportunities, and Threats to a business. They overcame the conventional framing effects and avoided getting into bad judgments by using this filtering and focusing process. Warren Buffett said: "If we have a strength, it is in recognizing when we are operating well within our circle of competence and when we are approaching the perimeter. Predicting the long-term economics of companies that operate in fast-changing industries is simply far beyond our perimeter."[15]

What about situations like a short term speculation with knowable shorter term advantages or catalysts? Can we intelligently increase our odds for successful predictions in an intelligently made speculation? We can start by applying Graham's ideas about eliminating companies and situations with unfavorable debt laden characteristics. That is one form of filtering. We can also try to avoid mistakes based upon irrational or emotional decisions. This is an internal form of self control and self-filtering.

Market Forces

Using a character called Mr. Market, Benjamin Graham taught his students two ways to deal with emotion in investing. First, he taught them the importance of avoiding mistakes based upon irrational or emotional decisions. Secondly, he taught them to recognize the opportunity created by irrational decisions made by the other party in the marketplace. The filter decision groups emphasize these behavioral ideas when applied to investment. However, remember that speculation does not guarantee the safety of principal invested. The best we can do is to approximate conditions that minimize potential loss.

In investing, experience and additive learning expands our own circles of competence. Charlie Munger calls this process the building of your own "Latticework of Mental Models."[16] Try to visualize putting our own knowledge base to work in an organized way in both speculation and investment.

Speculation Filter Number One

Develop an understanding of the most important factors needed in a speculative decision. Can speculators adopt these approaches to measuring both quantitative and qualitative values? Perhaps we can. Charlie Munger says "We all are learning, modifying, or destroying ideas all the time." Munger believes that the rapid destruction of our ideas when the time is right is one of the most valuable qualities we can acquire. He urges students to force themselves to consider arguments on the other side – inversion.[17]

Even though this example is over fifty years old, it is worth examining. In can be found in the 1960 Buffett Partnership Letter. It illustrates the quick recognition of additional business value in a business' special situation:

"Last year I mentioned a new commitment (Sanborn Map Co.) which involved about 25% of the assets of the various partnerships. Presently (1960), this investment is about 35% of assets. This is an unusually large percentage, but has been made for strong reasons. In effect, this company is partially an investment trust owning some thirty or forty other securities of high quality. Our investment was made and is carried at a substantial discount from asset value based on market value of their securities and a

conservative appraisal of the operating business...
There were no capital requirements to the
business... Thus, the investment portfolio
blossomed while the operating map business
wilted."[18]

Our understanding develops each time we add building
blocks to our mental models of reality, perceptions, and
misperceptions. Warren Buffett puts it this way: "Seek
whatever information will further your understanding of a
company's business."[19] On the other hand, Charlie
Munger likes to say: "We just throw some decisions into
the 'too hard' file and go onto others."[20] Munger advises
us to build our understanding like a "latticework of mental
models" based on facts with accurate and reality based
impressions.[21]

In investing, look for popular consumer brands and
potential "upward" pricing power. Also, keep in mind that

understanding a business and its products is a cumulative process. In intelligent speculation, specific examples like George Soros and John Paulson's speculations show that both men studied the macro characteristics of their speculative situation. Both men estimated the potential value of a mispricing correction. Both men had an idea of the herd of people involved. And, both men were looking for a catalyst that would bring about the force necessary for a pricing change. They operated at the scale of macro variables.

A Business Perspective

The scope of this book is looking at factors on a smaller scale. We benefit by starting to look at characteristics of a good business. For a quick start to understanding a productive business, take a look at a company's Free Cash Flow to the Firm, (FCFF). It is the amount of cash left over after the payment of the investments and taxes. (FCFF = NOP – Taxes – Net Investment – Net Change in

Working Capital). If FCFF is solid, then the business is serving customers and is making a profit. The key figures are the numbers seen after all the costs are accounted for.

For a quick start to eliminating "suspect companies," or ones we want to avoid in investing, look for bad terminology. In 2002, Buffett wrote "bad terminology is the enemy of good thinking." He warned us that companies or investment professionals using terms such as "EBITDA" and "pro forma," want us to unthinkingly accept concepts that are dangerously flawed. Charlie Munger has called EBITDA (Earnings Before Interest Taxes Depreciation and Amortization), "Bullshit Earnings."[22]

Benjamin Graham's Ideas

Ben Graham taught his students the golden key to successful investing. The key is to purchase shares in good businesses when market prices are at a large discount from underlying business values.   Benjamin Graham added three basic ideas that can enhance our investing framework.[23]   Graham's ideas can help us do reasonably well in stocks. According to Warren Buffett, Graham's three basic ideas are:

1. We should look at stocks as part ownership of a business,

2. We should look at market fluctuations in terms of his "Mr. Market" example and make them our friend rather than our enemy. We can learn to profit from market folly rather than participate in it.

3. The three most important words in investing are "Margin of Safety."

Ben Graham talked about safety in his last chapter of *The Intelligent Investor*. And, notice that "Margin of Safety" is the final determining step, of the "Four Filters" evaluation process. Knowing that some of his students would end up on Wall Street and engaged in speculation, Graham tried to get them to think about ways to do it more intelligently. By doing this, he was also trying to get them to think about how to filter out low-probability prospects.

The filter groups are an advancement encapsulating Graham's three fundamental investing ideas. These ideas have been enhanced further by adding investigation into "enduring competitive advantage"[24] and "able and trustworthy managers."[25] These four decision groups of thought and understanding are important for long-term investing success. Look for strengths, weaknesses, opportunities, threats, successes, and failures.

Graham said, "this final talk will address itself to speculation in relation to security analysis... there is a real difference between intelligent and unintelligent speculation, and that the methods of security analysis may often be of value in distinguishing between the two kinds of speculation… Speculative operations are all concerned with changes in price. In some cases the emphasis is on price changes alone, and in other cases the emphasis is on changes in value which are expected to give rise to changes in price."[26] Now you know why this book is called "Price To Value." Followers of this approach will also remember the importance of this P/V ratio in obtaining a margin of safety.

Graham's approach to "intelligent speculation" requires that a. the mathematical possibilities are not against the speculation. And, b. he suggested basing the measurement of these odds on experience and the careful weighing of relevant facts.

Focusing and Filtering

How do we find the relevant facts or factors? Warren Buffett cautions students to focus on their own circle of competence. Notice the filtering process within his statement here: "Draw a circle around the businesses you understand and then eliminate those that fail to qualify on the basis of value, good management, and limited exposure to hard times."[27] A big part of their evaluation process is to cast out businesses that are too difficult to understand. He and Charlie Munger understand that "the best business to own is one that over an extended period can employ large amounts of incremental capital at very high rates of return. The worst business to own is one that must, or will, consistently employ ever-greater amounts of capital at very low rates of return."[28] A good business has a loyal customer base. The wonderful ones will have some additional sort of pricing power. Adding a powerful driver to this process, Charlie Munger understood the importance of thinking about the "Wonderful Business"[29]

Shortly after purchasing Berkshire, they acquired a Baltimore department store called Hochschild Kohn. It was purchased through a retailing company called

Diversified Retailing that later merged with Berkshire Hathaway. They now consider this, as well as the original textile business purchase, an investing mistake.

Was it a speculative mistake? They were mistakes because they were businesses that did not have enduring competitive advantages. Therefore, they were destined for rough competition and diminishing profits. We too will make mistakes. However, we can learn from our mistakes. We can learn to limit our losses and maximize our gains. We can also learn from the "best practices" of the best practitioners of investing and speculation.

Both men admit they have learned from their mistakes. And, they have learned how to seek businesses with better economic prospects. Now, when buying companies or common stocks, they look for first-class businesses accompanied by first-class management. Buffett and Munger read the newspapers, think about a few of the big propositions, and go by their own sense of probabilities.[30] In 2002, Charlie Munger described the self-development process this way: "If you're going to be an investor, you're going to make some investments where you don't have all the experience you need. But if you keep trying to get a little better over time, you'll start to make investments that are virtually certain to have a good outcome. The keys are discipline, hard work, and practice. It's like playing golf -- you have to work on it." Practice speculating like the disciplined casino operation rather than the individual gambler. This alignment of odds is always framed to favor the house. "Think House Odds."

CHAPTER TWO
ADVANTAGES AND DISADVANTAGES

How can we develop an advantage when framing an intelligent approach to speculation? Minimizing the potential amount of loss is one thought. What about adding safety belts when thinking about counterparty risks and compressed time periods? First, look at risk minimization at the individual business level. Since the nature of capitalism is competition, a successful business needs to have "something special" in order to lead the pack with an advantage while fending off competitors. The absence of competitive advantage can signal a red light on an investment our business speculation. If we simplify our speculation model down to F=MA, or force equals mass times acceleration; the weakness of mass (critical information) or the weakness of acceleration (catalysts and catalytic conditions) will translate into real disadvantages.

In business investing, the two major types of competitive advantage are 1. a cost advantage, and 2. a differentiation advantage.[31] Our quest to find such businesses requires us to ask a lot of questions. What is the nature of the business over the next twenty years? Can we predict it with a high degree of accuracy? Can we imagine an enduring competitive advantage? Is it essential? Is there something special here? Is this advantage eroding? Are we being rational and realistic about our assessment?

Benjamin Graham urged his students to analyze the business. Sustainable Competitive Advantage is also called "favorable long-term prospects" or "enduring economic advantages." Sustainable Competitive Advantage comes from things that make a business difficult to copy. It is a barrier to entry that endures. A protected brand is such a barrier because it represents something unique and valued in the mind of a customer.

A valuable patent or trademark can give a firm a period of protected advantage, acting as a barrier to entry.

In intelligent speculation, we are looking for shorter term green light advantages. We look for factors that convey advantages. We want factors that convey favorable odds for success and facilitate a change in price or value. When we have sufficient information and catalytic conditions for a favorable change in price or value, we make our trade. However, one barrier can be forming the correct conclusion before the herd follows. This would be like timing a speculative change too early. In some trades, timing a move too early can lead to capital loss. So, forming the right mix of information and catalyst that varies from the herd's perceptions of price or value can facilitate a successful speculation. Michael Steinhardt called this a successful "variant perception." [32] It involves collecting data both symmetrically and asymmetrically, and forming a correct prediction. For his style of frequent trading, investing, and speculation, he needed to analyze a lot of dynamic variables.

Why not keep it simple? In investing, the common intellectual advantage of the investors from Graham-and-Doddsville is also their competitive advantage. Their search for a "Margin of Safety" is their advantage. Time and catalysts are of less importance for them. The Superinvestors of Graham-and-Doddsville did a better job in looking and finding discrepancies between the value of a business and the price of small pieces of that business in the market.[33] Finding quality bargains is their profitable "variant perception."[34] Add to this foundation of profitable bargain hunting by looking for a business with a big protective moat around it. They look for "Something special in peoples' minds." "Brands" "Technology" "Patent Protection" "Location" "Cost of Production" "Distribution System" "Local Service."[35] Look for the protective "Moat" around a business's economic castle.

Is it enduring or sustainable? Does it have a highly competitive system? Charlie Munger recommended the autobiography of Les Schwab, "Les Schwab Pride in Performance: Keep It Going." According to Munger, "Schwab ran tire shops in the Midwest and made a fortune by being shrewd in a tough business by having good systems." Another business, GEICO, was designed to be the low-cost operation in the marketplace of auto insurance.[36] GEICO's direct marketing gave it an enormous cost advantage over competitors that sold through agents. This is its barrier against competitors.

In speculation, a compressed time period often appears to be more important. In investing, time is the friend of the wonderful business, the enemy of the mediocre.[37] This ability to endure over time, in good times and in bad, and continue to earn a solid profit, is an important competitive advantage. And, sometimes, that comes about because of decent economics plus superior management who work to build a stronger moat. So, like the strong castle, the "Wonderful Business" usually has a strong, protective, and lasting moat around it.[38]

Talking about less competitive and weaker businesses, Warren Buffett said: "In many industries, differentiation simply can't be made meaningful. A few producers in such industries may consistently do well if they have a cost advantage that is both wide and sustainable." However, these are a few exceptional businesses. In many industries, such enduring winners do not exist. So, for the great majority of businesses selling "commodity" products, he believes that a depressing equation of business economics prevails. In his words, "a persistent over-capacity without administered prices (or costs) equals poor profitability."[39]

Buffett and Munger like strong brands like Coke and Gillette and Kraft. These companies have increased their worldwide shares of market in recent years. Their brand names, the attributes of their products, and the strength of their distribution systems give them competitive advantage. The average company, in contrast, does not have such protection.[40]

So what does this sustainable competitive advantage look like in numbers? Take a look at the Free Cash Flow, FCF, generated over time. And, look at ROE (Return on Equity) and NPM (Net Profit Margin).[41] Next, consider why the Coca-Cola Company is such a good business from an investor's point of view. Both Coke and Pepsi make products we enjoy. As an investor, I prefer the Coca-Cola Company. One reason is the amount of Free Cash Flow generated for every sale. Another reason is the amount of Free Cash Flow generated after expenses.

In another Berkshire Hathaway business, the Borsheim's jewelry subsidiary attracts business nationwide because of having several advantages that competitors can't match. Warren Buffett wrote that "the most important item in the equation is our operating costs, which run about 18% of sales compared to 40% or so at the typical competitor... Just as Wal-Mart, with its 15% operating costs, sells at prices that high-cost competitors can't touch and thereby constantly increases its market share, so does Borsheim's. NFM and Borsheim's follow "the same formula for success: (1) unparalleled depth and breadth of merchandise at one location; (2) the lowest operating costs in the business; (3) the shrewdest of buying, made possible in part by the huge volumes purchased; (4) gross margins, and therefore prices, far below competitors'; and (5) friendly personalized service with family members on hand at all times." [42]

How does practical competitive advantage tie in with current academic thought? In his book, "Competition Demystified", Bruce Greenwald of Columbia University presented a new and simplified approach to business strategy.[43] The conventional approach to strategy taught in business schools is based on Michael Porter's work. In Porter's model it is easy for students to get lost in a sophisticated model of competitors, suppliers, buyers, substitutes, and other players.[44] Greenwald warns us to not lose sight of the big question: "Are there barriers to entry that allow us to do things that other firms cannot?"

After establishing the importance of barriers to entry, Greenwald and Kahn argue that there are really only three sustainable competitive advantages; 1. Supply. A company has this edge when it controls an important resource: A company can have a proprietary technology that is protected by a patent. 2. Demand. A company can control a market because customers are loyal to it, either out of habit - to a brand name, for example - or because the cost of switching to a different product is too high. 3. Economies of scale. If your operating costs remain fixed while output increases, you can gain a significant edge because you can offer your product at lower cost without sacrificing profit margins. We can imagine a competitive advantage like the transcontinental railroad. It would be very expensive to reproduce.

Think Cost! What is the cost to me if this intelligently made speculative prediction fails to blossom? While many forces, both internal and external may be beyond our control, always try to imagine designing safety belts into your speculation model.

CHAPTER THREE
PEOPLE

In an election with two candidates, a population of people decide which individual would do a better job given the conditions at that time. In intelligent speculation, how does a person or group align the odds for success in their favor? Education of the proper facts and concepts is one universally accepted method. What about the ability and trustworthiness of the people involved in the investment or speculation? Surely, this should count for something of importance as well.

Investing Filter Number Three: Does the Business have Able and Trustworthy Managers?[45] Since a business is made up of human beings, the human capital invested in these organizations is important for its success. As investors, we should look for able and trustworthy and effective leadership within these companies. We depend on a group of thoughtful managers who are able to consider their situations and make wise decisions.

In intelligent speculation, it makes sense to deal with honest and honorable people rather than dishonest ones. Munger and Buffett have both said that "we can't do a good deal with a bad person." What about the market crowd during a speculative bubble? Has greed distorted our ability to price or value something? Perhaps the population of people who participate in such manias are misweighing the effects of their participation. Alternatively, it could be something as simple as playing in a social game with ignorance of the important facts. Social desirability bias is a term used to describe the tendency of people to reply in a manner that will be viewed favorably by others. We are social beings. So, we tend to follow social norms and try to fit in. In intelligent speculation, we must be prepared to act on our seemingly contrarian facts. Now, scientists continue to study the psychology of risk taking and gambling. They also study determinants that influence the shift from recreational gambling to problem gambling. We can see that individual psychological factors appear to motivate the problem laden gambler.[46] It will be interesting to see if future psychological research can identify winning and losing speculators. However, when pricing bubbles burst, a new sense of reality is generally recognized by all the participants.

At the individual business level, you may wonder how to better recognize an Able and Trustworthy Manager. Here are a few helpful clues. Able and Trustworthy Managers will build intrinsic value and competitive advantage. Able but greedy managers will steal from you. As a shareholder, and part owner of a business, do you want a manager taking more money from you than what was agreed upon in his or her contract?

Do you want a quick preliminary checklist for evaluating management? We can use this 4-step S.O.A.P. process that is taught to medical doctors; (Subjective, Objective, Assessment, Plan). And, we can use it as a screening tool for determining which people to watch. The process is better described in my "Four Filters Invention" book.

I urge the reader to use both feelings and facts in forming a more accurate impression of another person.

One easy way to spot suboptimal or "bad" managers is to calculate what percentage of the operating profits they are taking in total compensation. Have a "High Index of Suspicion" in formulating your preliminary diagnosis. As a shareholder, trust-but-verify that your managers are building "intrinsic value per share."[47] The market price will eventually follow.

As an owner or part-owner of a fine business, do you want a manager taking more money from your pocket and putting it into his or her pocket? We want to be associated with builders of "intrinsic value" rather than takers of "market value." In evaluating business acquisition candidates, Warren Buffett and Charlie Munger want their businesses run by managers they like, admire, and trust.[48] Look for managers who have Integrity, Intelligence, Energy, and Enthusiasm. For detailed examples, I refer you to Robert P. Miles book: "The Warren Buffett CEO." Bob Miles discusses many of the business managers at Berkshire Hathaway in greater detail.[49] These managers must have the ability to allocate capital efficiently within their own businesses.

Ben Graham also considered management. In his book "Security Analysis," Ben Graham admitted that it might be difficult to select unusually capable management. Since objective tests for management ability are rare, an investor often has to rely upon the reputation of a company's management. Graham was also aware of the psychological pressures facing managers. He made this comment about the temptation facing honest management: "While it should be emphasized that the overwhelming majority of management are honest, it must be emphasized also that loose or "purposive" accounting is a highly contagious disease... Manipulation of the reported earnings by the management even for the desirable purpose of maintaining them on an even keel is objectionable none the less because it may too readily lead to manipulation for more sinister reasons."

Buffett and Munger believe that the ability of management can dramatically affect the equity "coupons."[50] He wrote that "the quality of management affects the bond coupon only when management is inept or dishonest that payment of interest is suspended." When buying businesses or common stocks, they look for first-class businesses accompanied by first-class management. They value the previous owner's operational style. "We like to do business with someone who loves his business, not just the money that a sale will bring him (though we certainly understand why he likes that as well). When this emotional attachment exists, it signals that important qualities will likely be found within the business: honest accounting, pride of product, respect for customers, and a loyal group of associates having a strong sense of direction."[51]

Does an emotional attachment or passion signal anything in an intelligently made speculative decision? Perhaps there is a buildup of emotional attachment during the growth phase of a financial bubble. Then, like the impending burst of the housing and credit bubbles, levels of fear and default shift the market sentiment. Some people manage change better than others. The beauty of Munger's and Buffett's approach of associating with "Able and Trustworthy Managers" is simplicity. They do not have to coach great players at the peak of their games.

And, since many of these businesses already have a winning strategy, there is no need to develop new strategies.

In intelligent speculation, sometimes we bet against the prevailing attitudes of a population. Take a look at George Soros speech on his "Theory of Reflexivity."[52] According to Soros, we should look at the potential for reflexive change differently when we consider events which have thinking participants. In examining the current forces and potential forces involved in a market bubble, we must consider the effect of the participants' current thinking and possible future thinking. Phil Carret, who is discussed later in this book, was fascinated by the complexity of the forces which produce the ceaseless ebb and flow of security prices. While the majority of participants' thinking forces a buildup in speculative bubbles, there comes a point in time where sufficient conditions exist that can facilitate a change. If you wish to study Soros theory further, take a closer look at the interaction between the passive relationship he calls the "cognitive function" and the active relationship that he calls the "participating function." Next, look at the interaction between the two functions. Soros theory interprets social events as a never-ending historical process and not as an equilibrium situation. The conditions are better explained by using an analogy. The analogy is with water, which also can be found in nature in three conditions: as a liquid, a solid or a gas. In the case of water, the three conditions are related to temperature. Can you say "deal heat"? [53]

For readers not familiar with this term, take a look at "Winning" by Jack and Suzy Welch. There in chapter 14 on Mergers and Acquisitions, subtitled "Deal Heat and Other Deadly Sins", they define deal heat as the emotional excitement some managers feel compelling them to close a deal, even if the terms are unfavorable.

CHAPTER FOUR
PRICE AND VALUE

The Price to Value ratio is much more important than the price to earnings (p/e) ratio. Why? In both investing and speculating, having a sense of "intrinsic value" gives us a better sense of where to start. It also gives us a sense of the odds in our favor or the odds against us. In contrast, the earnings component of the p/e ratio is often manipulated by varying levels of debt. The intrinsic value of any asset is defined by the cash inflows and outflows - discounted at an appropriate interest rate - that can be expected to occur during the remaining life of the asset.[54]

Once we know the estimated intrinsic value, we can compare that figure with the market price and see if we are getting a bargain. If we are getting a bargain, this bargain is our Margin of Safety. "Margin of Safety" has been called the three most important words in investing by

Benjamin Graham and Warren Buffett.[55] This is the final filter of the Four Filters process.

We need a method of insuring safety. Insisting on a margin of safety helps us stack the odds favorably, in both speculation and investing. Purchasing something at a bargain price gives us this "margin of safety." It opens up the opportunity of using our remaining funds to purchase something else. It helps to protect us from market fluctuations and foolish losses. Warren Buffett and Charlie Munger believe this margin-of-safety principle, strongly emphasized by Ben Graham, is the cornerstone of investment success.[56] Can it be applied to framing an intelligent speculation decision? Can we add a safety belt to our speculation model? Yes. We can add in smaller safety measures if we design in a method to minimize our worst-case scenario loss.

After judging quality, how do we decide what price is a bargain? Buffett says that most analysts feel they must choose between two approaches: value and growth.[57] In Buffett and Munger's opinion, growth is a component in the calculation of value. Buffett said, ".. as one variable used in the calculation of value, growth's importance can range from negligible to enormous. And, growth can be both negative as well as positive."

Instead of growth, in intelligent speculation, we think more about the fast or slow maturation of a profitable event. The intelligent speculator also needs to know an approximate intrinsic value to his or her transaction. Without it, he or she is driving blindly into making a speculative decision. All reasonable people agree that driving with one good eye is much superior to driving blind. So, think about finding the important factors that can have a causal-like influence on a speculative change in price or value. Do we seek qualitative factors, quantitative factors, or both?

Ben Graham had a preference for the quantitative approach. He put it this way, "To my mind the prerequisite here is for the quantitative approach, which is based on the calculation of the probabilities in each case, and a conclusion that the odds are strongly in favor of the operation's success. It is not necessary that this calculation be completely dependable in each instance, and certainly not mathematically precise, but only that it be made with a fair degree of knowledge and skill. The law of averages will take care of minor errors and the many individual disappointments which are inherent in speculation."[58]

In sensible investing, you may wonder who came up with a formal way to calculate and reasonably estimate value. In 1938, John Burr Williams described the equation for value in his book, "The Theory of Investment Value."[59] Buffett summarized this as: "The value of any stock, bond, or business today is determined by the cash inflows and outflows - discounted at an appropriate interest rate - that can be expected to occur during the remaining life of the asset." Why discounted back to the present? Discount it back to the present because, over time, inflation tends to decrease the dollar's purchasing power.

In the section of his Chairman's Letter on "price attractiveness," Warren Buffett wrote "the (valuation) formula is the same for stocks as it is for bonds. Even so, there is an important, and difficult to deal with, difference between the two. A bond has a coupon and maturity date that define future cash flows; but, in the case of equities, the investment analyst must himself estimate the future "coupons."[60]

In a speculative decision, what is the value of the coupon we wish to receive? And, how much money are we willing to put at risk of loss in order to obtain that coupon? At the moment of purchase, will the market present us with good value at a bargain price? The big idea here is to look at a reasonable intrinsic value first. Think about the intrinsic value. Next, think about the price you are willing to pay to obtain that much value. In valuing a business as a whole, the main issue should not be about P/E (price to earnings) or P/B (price to book) or the Dividend Yield component. The main issue in business valuation is about finding and estimating the P/V (price to value ratio). "Price To Value" is the title of this book! This relative relationship of the intrinsic value of the business to the value obtained upon purchase is very important. In fact, Warren Buffett said that a high ratio of price to book value, a high price-earnings ratio, and a low dividend yield; are in no way inconsistent with a value purchase.[61]

If the investment prospect passes the "Four Filter" test of Understanding, Sustainable Competitive Advantage, and Able Trustworthy Managers, let's estimate a quantitative intrinsic value. Interestingly, Charlie Munger once stated: "Warren often talks about these discounted cash flows, but I've never seen him do one." Warren Buffett responded: "Its sort of automatic... It ought to just kind of scream at you that you've got this huge margin of safety."[62] He went on to state: "We define intrinsic value as the discounted value of the cash that can be taken out of a business during its remaining life. Anyone calculating intrinsic value necessarily comes up with a highly subjective figure. This figure will change both as estimates of future cash flows are revised and as interest rates move. Despite its fuzziness, however, intrinsic value is all-important and is the only logical way to evaluate the relative attractiveness of investments and businesses."

In intelligent speculation, take a look at the mathematical formula for Expected Value. Expected value (EV) = wager + (expected win – expected loss). It is the expected value of loss that must always be kept in mind. If we substitute the term like this: Expected Intrinsic Value = speculation cost + (expected speculation win – expected speculation loss); The expected value of loss in a speculation must still be weighed. Minimize your expected loss by designing safety belts into your speculation model. Avoiding the use of debt is one such safety measure. While readers can imagine limiting the amount of cash or stock used in an investment or speculation, sometimes the best safety measure can be inactivity.

Warren Buffett's Put Option Contracts

1. Understanding the Speculation

Berkshire <u>sold</u> 15- or 20-year put options on the S&P 500 and three foreign indexes. A put option (usually just called a "put") is a derivative and a financial contract between two parties. The contract writer is called the seller. The buyer acquires a short position with the right, but not the obligation, to sell the underlying instrument at an agreed-upon price (the strike price). The most widely-traded put options are on equities. However, they are traded on many other instruments such as interest rates and commodities. Buffett entered into "European" style put option contracts. This means they can only be exercised at expiration, and he won't need to worry about having to pay out the notional value before expiration. Berkshire collected a $4.9 billion option premium on $37.1 billion notional index options as of the date on his 2008 annual report.[63]

2. Advantages / Disadvantages

Buffett learned about the strengths and weaknesses of the Black-Scholes model from his experience with the LTCM meltdown in 1998. For 2008, the Black-Scholes model estimated a $10 billion liability, so Berkshire was required to show a $5.1 billion loss because of generally accepted accounting principles. However, as he says, "It's only the price on the final day that counts."

3. People Involved

In addition, he gets to use that $4.9 billion of cash for sensible reinvestment for the duration of the option. The put option contracts act as a form of insurance for buyers who want to limit their potential long-term losses on stocks. Berkshire will not have to make any payouts for any of these contracts until at least 2019. I believe that Berkshire Hathaway will be on the winning side of this bet in 2019.

4. Price and Value of the Speculation

Notice this interesting comment, "I believe each contract we own was mispriced at inception, sometimes dramatically so."

5. Catalysts and Conditions

Berkshire would have to pay money to the holders of the contracts if, on certain dates well in the future, four stock market indexes from around the world, including the S&P 500, are below where they were when the deals were made. With stocks plunging after the housing and credit bubble burst, in 2008-9 the value of the derivatives has also been falling. In 2009, $35.5 billion is potentially at risk from the contracts, but only if all four of the stock indexes involved drop to zero. If stocks eventually move higher by the end of the next decade, as Buffett expects, the contracts will be produce profits for Berkshire. The contracts' collateral requirements are, "under any circumstances, very minor." So, in effect, this was an intelligent speculation that the US economy will recover and grow a bit before 2019.

CHAPTER FIVE
CATALYSTS AND CONDITIONS

Charlie Munger said, "To understand a business, figure out what results it is achieving, why it is getting those results, and what could happen to change what is causing those results." Buffett and Munger are aware that we can easily fool ourselves. Therefore, they practice these mental checklist mechanisms to minimize the possibility of foolish errors.

What about economic conditions? Warren Buffett claims that he is "not a macro guy." He does not predict macroeconomic events or market conditions. He and Charlie Munger focus on individual business situations; and look for favorable prices relative to intrinsic value. Should we ignore macro catalysts? No. Big changes like the large recession of 2008 and 2009 bring about major price changes. In turn, this brings about mispriced golden opportunities and great quality bargains. However, remember that macroeconomic changes are things beyond our control. Like Ben Graham's mythical "Mr. Market," we do not try to control him. We try to profit from the mispricing opportunity that he may present to us.

One eager and studious speculator seized this opportunity with passion. In 2006, hedge fund manager John Paulson realized that the U.S. housing market and the value of subprime mortgages were grossly inflated. His variant perception was to sense that these values were headed for a major fall. While Paulson's background was in mergers and acquisitions, he was convinced this was his chance to make a big winning speculation. He and some colleagues studied the data. Paulson and other speculators such as Jeffrey Greene and Michael Burry began to bet heavily against risky mortgages and financial companies. Initially, their safety belt was testing their speculative bet on a smaller scale. At first, they lost millions of dollars as real estate and stocks continued to soar. However, in the summer of 2007, the markets began to implode. By the end of 2007, John Paulson had cleverly made the most profitable trade in financial history. He earned more than $15 billion for his firm. This now appears to be an intelligent speculation based on a much needed correction of inflated credit derivatives' values. Paulson made billions more in 2008 by transforming his variant perception.[64] He bet against the holders of the CDOs, Collateralized Debt Obligations.

The frequency and magnitude of major market changes are things we cannot control. The main option available to you is to surf or ride out the big wave. In both choices, safely control the board beneath you.

From an investment or speculative point of view, if a business passes a couple of decision filter groups, it is, by the process of elimination, entering a group of better performers. If this were a field of racing horses, movement forward along each step of the filters path, the prospect enters a subset group of "better than average" racing horses.

Sometimes, the potential forces for change appear to be near-boiling. When is it right to move forward with a speculation? The general answer would be to go forward when the overwhelming forces favor a good outcome with minimal risk of losses. In her biography of Warren Buffett, Snowball, Alice Schroeder wrote that Buffett was fearless in concentrating his bets. He kept buying into 1966 until he had spent $13 million on American Express. Buffett wrote, "We diversify substantially less than most investment operations. We might invest up to forty percent of our net worth in a single security under conditions **coupling** an extremely high probability that our facts and our reasoning are correct with a very low probability that anything could drastically change the underlying value of the investment."[65]

In intelligent speculation, the goals are similar. Couple a high probability that our information advantage and our reasoning is correct, with a low probability that anything could drastically change the value of our variant perception. Some do this consciously and some do it seemingly semiconsciously. Either way, building in a "margin of safety" or "minimization of amount of loss" makes good sense. Consider the amount of potential loss from each speculative bet. Then, try to design safety belts into each carefully made speculation.

Some of you might want to use debt and leverage your speculation. Debt reminds me of nitroglycerin. A little bit may be helpful. Moderate and larger amounts are dangerous. I had thought about writing about money borrowing rates in this section. Such a discussion would have included the Federal Funds Rate, Primary Discount Rate, Secondary Discount Rate, and the Broker Call Rate.

It could have also included a look into the cost of holding and investing insurance float money. Instead, I refer readers to other books that look into WACC, the weighted average cost of capital. A business' assets are financed by either debt or equity. WACC is the average of the costs of these sources of financing, each portion of which is weighted by its respective use in the given situation.

In my view, the intelligent speculator should generally avoid debt. How dangerous is debt? The low cost of funds motivated some traders to run wild with uneconomic and unintelligent speculations. Then, pricing bubbles grow and eventually burst. In the 1987 crash, the tumult began as the Federal Reserve raised the discount rate over that Labor Day weekend.

Alice Schroeder wrote that Warren Buffett views debt as almost sinful. She mentioned that there was one time when he advocated a its use. When Berkshire was selling at $40 a share Buffett thought it was so cheap that he was willing to have his sisters borrow an extraordinary ninety-five percent of the purchase price to buy it.

If you are tempted to use debt, consider the possibility of permanent and magnified loss, and use extreme caution.

CHAPTER SIX
TWO EXAMPLES

Operations not promising safety of principal and a satisfactory return are speculative. In this chapter, I give one sparkling example of a winning speculation and one tragic example of a losing speculation. These two examples are framed inside the simple "intelligent speculation model" proposed earlier.

We will look back at the losing speculation of Long Term Capital Management (LTCM) and the winning speculation of John Paulson's Great Housing Bubble Trade. How do they fit with our model? Did they truly understand the odds and did they have the discipline to bet only when the odds were in their favor?[66] Examine the basic framework of decision filter groups and you be the judge.

LTCM's Losing Speculation

1. Understanding the Speculation

Roger Lowenstein's book, "When Genius Failed" is the tale of what happened when an elite group of investors ran Long Term Capital Management. LTCM was a company that tried to mathematically manage risk and use high leverage to create wealth. The founders included two Nobel Prize-winning economists, Myron Scholes and Robert C. Merton. Scholes and Merton, along with the late Fischer Black, developed the Black-Scholes formula for option pricing. LTCM exploited small arbitrage opportunities on a big scale. Scholes stated that "LTCM acted like a giant vacuum cleaner sucking up nickels that everyone else had overlooked." The strategy worked well for a couple of years before failing dramatically.

2. Advantages / Disadvantages

Fancy mathematics from the Black-Scholes option pricing model proved to be both an advantage and a disadvantage. Early on, their formulas worked for arbitrage. Later, a big event triggered a run of failure. High Leverage proved to be catastrophic. LTCM placed their investors' money in a variety of trades simultaneously. It was a volatile hedging strategy designed mathematically to minimize the possibility of loss. When a 1998 default in Russia set off a global financial storm, Long-Term's models failed.

3. People Involved

In 1993, John Meriwether, a former partner at Salomon Brothers, established a smart group of bond arbitrage experts. This group included a pair of Nobel Prize winners. LTCM had its origins in an Arbitrage Group put together by Meriwether at Salomon Brothers. He was a successful bond market trader with prestige and influence within that firm. Although he was a shrewd trader he was also good at choosing and managing talented people. Meriwether recruited Eric Rosenfeld and William Lasker from the faculty at Harvard. He also hired Victor Haghani, who trained in finance at the London School of Economics. Lawrence Hilibrand was trained in finance at M.I.T. and Gregory Hawkins had a Ph.D. in finance from M.I.T. While at Salomon, Meriwether's Arbitrage Group was so successful at earning profits that they were able to demand a change in the way they were compensated. This created envy and resentment among the other groups at Salomon.

4. Price and Value of the Speculation

At Long-Term Capital, Meriwether & Co. believed that their computer software models could manage risk with near mathematical certainty. [67] Long-Term's traders borrowed with little concern about the high level of leverage. In raising funds Meriwether created the category of Strategic Investors who invested at least $100 million. He was successful in bringing in some of the top financial organizations in the world into LTCM despite expensive fees. The typical hedge funds charged 20 percent of profits earned plus a one percent of an investor's assets as fees. In contrast LTCM charged 25 percent of profits and levied a 2 percent fee on assets. Despite the heavy fees and long term commitment LTCM was able to raise $1.25 billion. At first, Long-Term's models worked and both private investors and central banks invested more money. Their system relied on a high volume of trades, but it lacked the ability to anticipate a sudden macro change.

5. Catalysts and Conditions

When a default in Russia set off a global financial storm that Long-Term Capital's models had not anticipated, its portfolios sank in market value. In five weeks, the professors went from rich geniuses to discredited failures. Global investors panicked about risk. They wanted more certainty and they fled the unpredictable markets for quality securities, ones with a higher degree of certainty. Thus higher differentials for the riskier securities did not stop the flight to quality securities. For LTCM, whose models bet on the re-instatement of equilibrium conditions, it was a ruinous time. The firm began to lose hundreds of millions of dollars each day. Events such as earthquakes, defaults, political revolution and so forth do bring instantaneous changes in prices. The models used by LTCM did not allow for this type of risk.

Although the LTCM traders took a large number of separate positions, there was no benefit in risk-reduction through diversification in this financial crisis. Why? Because most of the separate transactions were the same bet on the stabilization of the markets and a return to equilibrium. With the firm about to go under, its staggering $100 billion balance sheet threatened to drag down markets around the world. Fearing that the financial system of the world was in danger, the Federal Reserve Bank summoned Wall Street's leading banks to underwrite a bailout. On September 23, 1998, Goldman Sachs, AIG, and Berkshire Hathaway offered to buy out the fund's partners for $250 million. Plus, they offered to add $3.75 billion and operate LTCM within Goldman's own trading division. The offer was stunningly low to LTCM's partners because their firm had been worth $4.7 billion earlier that year. Buffett gave Meriwether one hour to accept the deal and the time period lapsed before a deal could be worked out. Seeing no options left the Federal Reserve Bank of New York organized a bailout of $3.6 billion by the major creditors to avoid a wider financial collapse.

John Paulson's Winning Speculation[68]

1. Understanding the Speculation

Paulson & Co., Inc. profited from the subprime mortgage crisis. It had assets under management of $12.5 billion in June of 2007. Most of this was raised from institutions. This amount climbed to $36 billion by November 2008 because Paulson & Co. capitalized on the problems in the foreclosure and mortgage backed securities (MBS) markets.

2. Advantages / Disadvantages

Paulson was not a mortgage or real estate expert. He did not have much of a background in the derivatives, the credit-default swaps (CDS) that he used to make the big bets. His advantage was to believe, learn, wait, and act on his variant perception.

3. People Involved

John Paulson spent a career on Wall Street underappreciated as an investor. He had slowly built up his hedge fund. By 2005 he started getting nervous about the overpriced housing market and the proliferation of subprime mortgages. Subprime mortgages were bundled into complex derivative instruments known as MBS, mortgage backed securities. Paulson and others started to think about how to bet against this price and value mispricing. Paolo Pellegrini helped John Paulson make this great trade. His study of the data helped reveal the changing indicators to them. In 2007, Paulson made $15 billion for his firm. In 2008, he transformed the trade into a bet against financial firms. This generated another $5 billion.

4. Price and Value of the Speculation

The oversupply of lower grade subprime mortgages fed a house building frenzy and home price inflation. While one needs to get the timing right in order for a bet for change to be profitable, there is usually no incentive to bet against a bubble. In the middle of '06, Paulson and others started making such trades. To this select few, they sensed that the conditions were favorable for a massive downturn in the housing market and subprime securities. The derivatives known as MBS or mortgage backed securities were complex and dangerously overvalued.

5. Catalysts and Conditions

When was the catalytic moment of change? This group of successful traders started having worries about the state of the economy and the housing market in 2005. [69]   They wanted to buy puts on the S&P 500, but found them too expensive. So they started buying these CDS contracts, which are basically insurance policies on debt. The CDS prices were perceived to be very cheap. So, Paulson and Pellegrini studied these CDS contracts. They decide that they wanted to raise a fund to do this trade on a large scale. If Paulson could raise a specific hedge fund dedicated to betting against housing, he could make a fortune. Others had interesting arguments against this perception. The contracts were hard to trade, and the government might act quickly to stop a broad financial collapse.

Paulson and others started their bets in the middle of 2006, and they did not work out well early on. However, in the winter and spring of 2007 the indexes Paulson was betting against start to move downward dramatically. His biggest gains were in '07, but in 2008, he was still bearish on housing. He switched to buying credit-default swaps on the institutions that were peddling subprime mortgages, like Bear Stearns. Others soon accepted this variant perception and followed. Now, Bear Stearns is history. Paulson made a brilliant bet shorting subprime.

The Bear Stearns Companies, Inc. was a global investment bank and securities trading firm until its collapse and sale to JPMorgan Chase in 2008. Bear Stearns pioneered the securitization and asset-backed securities markets. Interestingly, as investor losses mounted in 2006 and 2007, the company actually increased its exposure to mortgage-backed derivatives. In March 2008, the Federal Reserve Bank of New York provided an emergency loan to try to stop a sudden collapse of the company. The company could not be saved, and it was sold to JPMorgan Chase. In January 2010, JPMorgan discontinued use of the Bear Stearns name.

Can a "margin of safety" be built into a speculative decision? Successful speculators would say that some "safety belts" can be added to intelligently made speculations. Having important controllable factors on your side can favor the probabilities for a good outcome. If the macro economy was not in a recession, and there was no oversupply of houses, land developers would be thinking of ways to develop and build "spec" homes. In normal economic conditions, they would design and sell such spec homes with an ideal mix of product features, price, place, and promotions. Understanding the economics, advantages, disadvantages, people, prices, values, and catalysts involved in framing a speculative decision is the foundation of making a risk-minimizing decision.

Speculator beware! Be aware to not invest nor speculate if the odds are not in your favor. Charlie Munger believes in this tactic. He had enlisted in the Army a year after Pearl Harbor. Alice Schroeder wrote that Munger augmented his army pay by playing poker. "He found he was good at it. It turned out to be his version of the racetrack. He said he learned to fold fast when odds were bad and bet heavily when they were good, lessons he would use to advantage later in life." [70]

A thoughtful investment operation, on thorough analysis, promises safety of principal and a satisfactory return. Operations not promising safety of principal and a satisfactory return are speculative. In either operation, I believe that Charlie Munger's statement is appropriate: "You have to understand the odds and have the discipline to bet only when the odds are in your favor."[71]

Even if the odds seem to be in your favor, remember the warning Benjamin Graham gave us in The Intelligent Investor: "In most periods the investor must recognize the existence of a speculative factor in his common-stock holdings. It is his task to keep this component within minor limits, and to **be prepared financially and psychologically for adverse results** that may be of short or long duration."

CHAPTER SEVEN
Phil Carret's Ideas

Philip Carret founded Pioneer Fund in 1928, six years before Ben Graham wrote the 1st edition of Security Analysis. Carret also wrote a useful and enlightening book called "The Art of Speculation." And, Warren Buffett stated that Philip Carret "had the best truly long-term investment record of anyone I know."

What made Carret so successful in investing? I asked Frank Betz, of Carret Zane Capital Management, a similar question. Frank shared a partner's desk with Phil Carret as his personal assistant from the mid-eighties until Phil's death in 1998. Carret was then over age 101, and he was still commuting most days from his Scarsdale home to the mid-town NYC office of Carret and Company that he founded in 1962. There he was still functioning fully in the management of client portfolios. Betz recalled that

Phil was a voracious reader not only of dozens of corporate annual reports and daily newspapers, but of an eclectic variety of books ranging from philosophy, history, biography and economic subjects. Phil Carret always claimed the most useful information he gleaned from this was from his concentration on the detailed footnotes appended to annual reports.

While Frank was already a long experienced money center banker, analyst, and investor when he was recruited to work for Carret by Phil's son Donald, I wanted to know how this interaction affected his own approach to investing. Frank believes that "working with Phil Carret, significantly sharpened my senses."

Frank Betz also remembers that Carret would warn others against following fads in investing, and he often cited one of the most important characteristics of successful investors is patience. In the preface of his book, Phil

Carret wrote, "The man who looks upon speculation as a possible means of avoiding work will get little benefit from this book. It is written rather for the man who is fascinated by the complexity of the forces which produce the ceaseless ebb and flow of security prices, who wishes to get a better understanding of them."

"Successful speculation requires capital, courage and judgment. The speculator himself must supply all three. Natural good judgment is not enough. The speculator's judgment must be trained to understand the multitudinous facts of finance." Like mine, it was Carret's hope that his book would assist his readers.

At the 1996 Berkshire Hathaway Annual Meeting, Warren Buffett said: "The main thing is to find wonderful businesses, like Phil Carret, who's here today, always did. He's one of my heroes, and that's an approach he's used. If you've never met Phil, don't miss the opportunity. You'll learn more talking with him for fifteen minutes than by listening to me here all day."

Let us take a brief look at Carret's somewhat contrarian view on oil. "Oil is produced in thousands of oil fields on every continent in the world. The temporary absence from the market of a single country - even a country as important to oil as Iraq or Kuwait - will have only a temporary effect. Other oil producers can boost their output quickly. And in the United States, we have abundant supplies of natural gas, which can serve as a substitute for oil to a considerable extent."

More importantly, take a look at Phil Carret's "12 Commandments of Investing":

1. Never hold fewer than 10 different securities covering five different fields of business;

2. At least once every six months, reappraise every security held;

3. Keep at least half the total fund in income producing securities;

4. Consider (dividend) yield the least important factor in analyzing any stock;

5. Be quick to take losses and reluctant to take profits;

6. Never put more than 25% of a given fund into securities about which detailed information is not readily and regularly available;

7. Avoid inside information as you would the plague;

8. Seek facts diligently, advice never;

9. Ignore mechanical formulas for value in securities;

10. When stocks are high, money rates rising and business prosperous, at least half a given fund should be placed in short-term bonds;

11. Borrow money sparingly and only when stocks are low, money rates low and falling and business depressed;

12. Set aside a moderate proportion of available funds for the purchase of long-term options on stocks in promising companies whenever available.

We see that Phil Carret exercised safety-based commandments. And, the last one appears to be targeted towards "intelligent speculation." There, he advised setting aside a proportion of available funds for long-term options on stocks in promising companies whenever available. With careful study and patience, Carret knew he could predict good outcomes. Philip Carret died on May 28, 1998, at age 101.

CHAPTER EIGHT
A Bill Ruane Case Sample

Bill Ruane and the Ruane, Cunniff & Goldfarb team of analysts provide an interesting case of an intelligent investment with speculative features. This case on Progressive Insurance illustrates the "team based research culture" created by Bill Ruane to develop differential insights. The firm's unique research process and collective focus on an idea lead to insights different from those in the marketplace. This provided Ruane's team a unique opportunity to exploit stock market inefficiencies. If the future of investing at Berkshire Hathaway is shared by a team of four or five managers, I think this case and their team approach is worth contemplation.

Thanks to Paul Lountzis of Lountzis Asset Management in Wyomissing, Pennsylvania, readers have this added case example worth studying.

William J. Ruane was widely respected as both a talented investment manager and philanthropist. Bill graduated with the famous Harvard Business School Class of 1949 that included, Lester Crown, Harry Figgie, Marvin Traub, John Shad, Thomas Murphy, James Burke and Roger Sonnabend and Joe Amaturo.

Bill Ruane worked as a stockbroker at Kidder, Peabody. After reading two important books, "Where Are the Customers' Yachts?" and "Security Analysis," Ruane attended Ben Graham's class. Bill Ruane met Warren Buffett at an investment seminar led by Benjamin Graham. They became lifelong friends. Ruane headed into the 1960's with confidence yet humility. These traits, along with his keen intellect, served him well. Two of his investment successes in the 1960's were Capital Cities Broadcasting (run by his Harvard Business School Classmate Tom Murphy) and the Walt Disney Company.

In 1969, Ruane and Richard Cunniff took their shop out of Kidder, Peabody to continue managing private accounts. They also started the Sequoia Mutual Fund to handle smaller investors including many referred by Warren Buffet. Buffett advised associates to invest with Ruane after he closed out his initial Buffett partnerships.

Bill Ruane's first few years as in independent investment advisor coincided with the worst investment climate since the Great Depression. Stocks were trounced in 1973 and 1974. Bill persisted and his firm bought many bargains during that time. This lead to outstanding results.

The Sequoia Fund routinely outperformed the S&P 500 index and has been one of the top performing mutual funds. The successful firm was renamed Ruane, Cunniff, and Goldfarb in 2004 to acknowledge the contributions of Robert D. Goldfarb, who had been with the firm since 1971.

1. Understanding the Investment/Speculation

In 1993, Bill Ruane and his team at Ruane Cunniff & Goldfarb became interested in the Progressive Insurance Company. Progressive, a small auto insurance company, had achieved outstanding long term financial results which attracted the team. Progressive operated in the non-standard or high risk segment of the auto insurance market. The entire team began collectively focusing upon understanding the key qualitative characteristics that generated those outstanding financial metrics and how durable and sustainable they were over the long term.

Progressive's stock price had peaked in October of 1993 and began its 30% decline through March of 1994. The stock's decline was due to Progressive's announcement that they were going to raise their combined ratio target to 96% from the mid 80% range, hence potentially reducing their short term operating profit by 67%. Progressive's unusual profitability attracted several competitors.

Progressive aggressively exercised its competitive advantages in pricing segmentation and claims by offering lower prices to remove that pricing umbrella and thwart competitors. Lower prices led to rapid growth and rising competitive barriers, which long term represented an outstanding investment opportunity particularly after a 30% stock price decline.

Progressive was also contemplating several new growth initiatives including entering the much larger standard auto insurance market which at $100 billion was over six times the size of the non-standard market as well as selling their products through the direct distribution channel, while still maintaining their legacy independent agency channel.

Bill Ruane and his team believed Progressive was a mispriced bargain and the firm purchased almost 9 million shares at discounted prices about half for the Sequoia

Fund and the other half for its private accounts. With a 3 for 1 stock split in April of 2002, and a 4 for 1 stock split in 2006, the results have been outstanding with Progressive's stock having appreciated over 10 times from its 1994 low.

2. Advantages / Disadvantages

Advantages:

- Superior pricing segmentation.

- Superior claims.

- Outstanding management team both operationally and financially.

- New growth opportunity in much larger standard market.

- New growth opportunity in direct distribution channel.

Disadvantages:

- Greater competition in standard auto insurance market.

- Execution risks in entering both the standard auto insurance market and direct distribution channel.

- Alienating existing independent agency channel and creating channel conflict.

- Maintaining high standards in hiring required with growth of over 30% per annum.

- Losing strategic and financial focus with several new initiatives.

3. People Involved

The team was led by Bob Goldfarb and included Carley Cunniff, Greg Alexander, Jon Brandt, Kirk Hosfelt, Andy Kneeter, Tania Pouschine and Paul Lountzis. The firms' unique collective focus working together on a singular idea utilized a complementary set of skills that yielded outstanding results.

In the 1996 Sequoia Fund annual report, Bill Ruane wrote: "Rounding out our research team are four highly discerning analysts, Kirk Hosfelt, Andy Kneeter, Paul Lountzis and Tania Pouschine, who work hand in hand with us with a primary focus on developing an in-depth qualitative understanding of the products, organizations and managements of our portfolio companies. Tania is particularly astute in the thoughtful appraisal of company managements and Kirk excels in getting at the nuts and bolts of how a business really works. Andy and Paul do an outstanding job concentrating on developing extensive business information sources to shed light on key business issues."

4. Price and Value of the Speculation

Did Wall Street misprice the value of Progressive Insurance? Why did the market price of Progressive drop? Wall Street sold off the stock in late 1993 and early 1994 as the company announced it would reduce its operating profitability by 67% raising its combined ration from about 83 to a target of around 96. This means that the ratio of losses plus expenses were growing relative to the earned premium. However, remember that this strategic spending was an intentional move to grow the business.

Ruane's team shared their research within the firm and discussed the strengths and weaknesses of this growth initiative. The team made several trips to Progressive's largest client states, in terms of premiums written, including Florida and Ohio.

Wall Street's short term focus did not recognize the long term opportunity for Progressive entering both the standard auto insurance market as well as the direct distribution channel for its products. Over the longer term view, the firm believed that Progressive would be able to apply its expertise in pricing to standard auto insurance and create an additional outlet for distributing its products through the direct channel. The direct channel was the most rapidly growing portion, and it provided the firm with another customer segment. With a long term view they were able to gain confidence in rapid growth that would result from much lower prices. Progressive aimed to meet that demand by continuing to hire great people and maintain its competitive advantage in pricing and claims.

Several risks mentioned above came into play and Progressive was able to overcome them and succeed. First, Progressive's non-standard insurance product was distributed exclusively through independent agents. Progressive had decided to begin lowering commissions from 15% to 10%. It was requiring agents to invest in technology to work with Progressive's products. Progressive was also going to begin distributing their product direct to consumers. These factors raised the issue of whether these independent agents would begin moving business away from Progressive. After the teams' research was completed, they concluded that Progressive's core non-standard business was safe because prices were still typically 10-15% or more lower than competitors. If agents did not mention Progressive prices to prospective buyers of such high priced insurance the customer would shop it and by leveraging agents against agents. Customers would get some agents to give them a Progressive quote. The winning agent would figure that he would rather get a 10% commission on a $4,000 policy than nothing at all.

Second, Progressive was the only insurer for many types of risks, so agents needed to keep them. Progressive also excelled in technology. So, this made them the easiest to deal with. For all the reasons confirmed in the marketplace, Ruane's team felt secure that Progressive's core business would continue to thrive and generate positive cash flows. In turn, this enabled Progressive to move into standard auto insurance as well as enter the direct distribution channel.

Ruane's team's second core question was whether Progressive could succeed in standard insurance. This was a whole new market with much more competition from State Farm and Allstate. This new market brought different pricing segmentation. It required a new channel of independent agents to write this product. Progressive was also simultaneously entering the direct distribution channel. With this dynamic period having lots of moving parts and new strategies, Progressive took on a greater level of operational and financial risk.

Ruane's team found several independent agents that were writing meaningful amounts of standard business with Progressive. Many insurance agents repeatedly claimed that they needed a high quality standard insurance company they could trust that provided high quality

114

products. They needed a business partner that had a commitment to the business, while having smaller minimum requirements. At that time, the larger players like Aetna, Cigna, Travelers, etc. were requiring high minimums to do business with them.

Some required business of over $1 million and above to conduct business with independents. Several insurance companies did not have the expertise in pricing, claims, reserving that Progressive had. Some insurers came into and out of this market lacking service and pricing consistency.

Ruane's team became convinced that there was a unique opportunity for Progressive to build their standard business through agents as well as the direct distribution channel. Ultimately, it all worked out and Progressive has succeeded in standard insurance, as well as building an outstanding direct distribution model that is exceeded only by Geico. The team was able to leverage these insights into a large position that paid off handsomely for the clients of both Ruane, Cunniff & Goldfarb as well as their Sequoia Fund.

5. Catalysts and Conditions

Progressive Insurance had intentionally lowered prices and attempted to grow the business in both Nonstandard and Standard insurance offerings. As a consequence, their short term profitability decreased. And, the stock market priced the business lower.

The catalyst was Progressive announcing that they were going to reduce their operating profitability by 67% and the stock price declined by 30% from late 1993 to early 1994. That price decline became an opportunity to purchase a very good company with growth prospects.

The research team concluded that each of the critical issues were addressed. First, Progressive would continue to maintain a leading market share with its non standard products within independent agents. Second, Progressive's entry into the standard auto insurance market was already being successfully sold by several agents and they believed it would continue to grow. Third, Progressive's entry into direct distribution was beginning to gain a small bit of traction in Florida where they had been experimenting with this channel for years.

Ruane's team concluded that Progressive's future was bright and they would continue to prosper in their core non standard business as well as succeed in entering both the standard auto insurance market and the direct distribution channel.

Today, Progressive is one of the top 5 auto insurers in the country and has built a solid presence in the standard auto insurance market as well as being the number two player behind Geico in the direct distribution channel.

This Progressive case sample illustrates the necessary patience, discipline, and conviction to make an investment after a 30% price decline. Like all great investors including, Ben Graham, Warren Buffett, Charlie Munger, and Phil Carret, Bill Ruane had patience, discipline, and with the research team generating differential insights that provided Bill with the courage and conviction to make a large investment commitment. Once his intelligently framed perception was backed up by solid qualitative and quantitative data, Bill Ruane had the conviction to step up to the plate with a sizable position.

CHAPTER NINE
A Case From Joe Koster

This case comes to the reader from a friend of mine, Joe Koster. Joe is a young analyst for Chanticleer Holdings, Inc. in Charlotte, North Carolina. I read a couple of his blogs on the internet a couple years ago, and realized that he understood the difference between intelligent investing and intelligent speculation. Then, about a year ago, I was passing thru Charlotte and had the chance to talk with him.

I was impressed with his knowledge of the Graham-Buffett-Munger value investing philosophy. And, I was impressed with this young man's temperament. Here is his "intelligent speculation" case in his own words.

1. Understanding the Speculation

Winmill & Co. Incorporated ("Winmill"), through its subsidiaries, provides investment management, and shareholder and distribution services to sponsored investment companies. It offers advisory, advertising, and brokerage services for open end mutual funds, as well as for closed-end funds. It is traded on the Pink Sheets (WNMLA.PK).

The significant portions of Winmill's value are its stake in Bexil Corp. ("Bexil"), which it also runs, and its fund-management business. Bexil is also traded on the Pink Sheets (BXLC.PK) and its balance sheet and value is almost entirely in cash (roughly $38 per Bexil share). It is looking to make an acquisition with that cash. The biggest portion of the fund-management business is through Winmill's management of the Midas Fund. As of this writing, Winmill currently has over $150 million in assets under management.

There appears to be a large gap between the current price and intrinsic value of Winmill & Co. If one includes the company's share of the cash on Bexil's balance sheet, Winmill is trading for less than the net cash value per share, after subtracting all liabilities.

2. Advantages / Disadvantages

Advantages:

- Easy to understand business and thesis for value.
- A business model where the infrastructure in place would allow additional revenue – should revenue and assets under management grow – to flow largely to the bottom line.

- Management that owns a significant number of shares.
- Large margin of safety.
- Potential catalyst in place.

Disadvantages:

- Thinly-traded stock on the Pink Sheets.
- Uncertainty as to the availability and timing of financial information.
- Lack of an independent board of directors.

3. People Involved

The management team most prominently consists of the father-son combo of Bassett (Chairman) and Tom Winmill (CEO). They have a significant stake in both Winmill & Co. and Bexil Corp., so their interests are fairly well aligned with shareholders. They've proved they can be capable evaluators of value, as is evidence by their investment with Bexil in York Insurance Services Group, which they sold in 2006 for about a 17x cash on cash return, with dividends included, over a 4-year holding period.

4. Price and Value of the Speculation

As of this writing (early March 2010), the last trade of Winmill's shares was at $3.00 per share. As of September 30, 2009, tangible book value per share was $5.63. Of note in this tangible book value per share number is the fact that the investments are valued at market prices at the end of the September 2009 quarter. Although Winmill's investments in Foxby Corp. and Tuxis Corp. may be valid to value at market prices, Winmill's investment in Bexil is much easier to value since Bexil is currently just a pile of cash as the company waits to find an appropriate acquisition. Bexil's market price at the end of the third quarter of 2009 was $24.50, compared to a cash-per-share value of approximately $38. Making this adjustment, Winmill's tangible book value per share would become $7.64. I believe this is the minimum value of Winmill's shares, as it also gives no credit and no value to an investment-management business that has over $150 million in assets under management and a decent long-term track record. If a conservative value for the investment management business is considered, I believe the value of Winmill falls somewhere in the range of $8.50 - $10.00 per share.

Furthermore, what makes this speculation intelligent is the downside protection inherent in Winmill from its balance sheet. The company has no long-term debt and – after considering Winmill's look-through share of Bexil's cash and then subtracting all liabilities – a net cash per share value of about $5.72. So at $3.00 per share, one can buy a dollar of cash for approximately 52 cents ($3.00/$5.72).

Although there are certainly risks with Winmill (see the 'Disadvantages' section above), there appears to be a significant discrepancy between market price and intrinsic value.

5. Catalysts and Conditions

For most of January 2010, Winmill traded between $2.28 and $2.35 per share. Winmill then began to trade higher after the company issued a press release showing its financial situation as of September 30, 2009. The previous financial update by the company covered the quarter ending on September 30, 2007, so there were 2 years between financial updates. As the company is listed on the Pink Sheets, it is not required to file periodic updates. However, the company has received some pressure from at least one shareholder, which may have helped to prompt the company to update its current financial numbers. If this trend continues, more people may gain confidence that the company will continue to report and this may be a catalyst for the company's shares to approach a market price that more closely reflects intrinsic value.

Also, because a decent portion of Winmill's value is contained in Bexil's shares, which currently trade below the cash balance that makes up almost the entire business, an acquisition by Bexil of a business or other assets could potentially serve as a catalyst for Winmill shares as well, although the timing of this catalyst is unpredictable.

To quote legendary investor Seth Klarman, "Be sure that you are well compensated for illiquidity – especially illiquidity without control – because it can create particularly high opportunity costs." Winmill & Co. – and Bexil too, for that matter – are very illiquid and control rests in the hands of company insiders, but I believe the extreme discrepancy between price and value makes this speculation an intelligent one.

Final Note

In doing research for this book, I have learned that intelligent speculation should be made with safety, structure, and value in mind. So the idea of framing such decisions seem helpful. Risk should be viewed as the permanent loss of capital. Valuation should include an estimation of both win and loss scenarios. A causality perspective may be superior to a correlation perspective.

This book proposed a sensible model for framing an intelligent speculation decision. Imagine the value of improving your decision framing ability. Consider that some factors are controllable and some are not. Account for forces that are in favor of and forces that are against speculation success. Also account for the hidden force of sudden changes in events, so that potential losses can me minimized.

Like business investing, account for an economic understanding, advantage versus disadvantage, people, price versus value, and catalyst/condition factors. Evaluate the natural tendencies of these factors. Consider the competitive forces at play. Which factors are controllable and which are not? What is the significance of event time, frequency, and magnitude in the catalyst/conditions section? Herein lies the value of simplicity over complexity. Think about the effects, biases, decisions, people, and prices being paid.

Is the speculation being analyzed intelligently or is it being motivated by greed and emotional factors? Is there deal heat in this market? While a true "margin of safety" may not be feasible, are there safety belts, cushions, parachutes, locks, alarms, or insurance built into our speculation? We must always consider that the odds may favor inactivity. Think. Inactivity may be the wisest choice of all.

APPENDIX

Human biases listed at Wikipedia.org (as of 02/06/2010)

This section is dedicated to Charles T. Munger, who has had a life-long fascination with cognitive biases. These biases were found on a wikipedia.org web page labeled "List of Cognitive Biases." They were rearranged using the sort feature of Microsoft's Excel program. They are included here to stimulate your thinking into different ways that we can reduce our speculative thinking mistakes. Readers who wish to learn more about the scientists and theoreticians who discovered these concepts are encouraged to start their research at: http://en.wikipedia.org/wiki/List_of_cognitive_biases

Actor-observer bias: The actor-observer bias is a term that refers to a tendency to attribute one's own action to external causes, while attributing other people's behaviors to internal causes. The actor-observer bias tends to be more pronounced in situations where the outcomes are negative. People tend to make different attributions depending upon whether they are the actor in a situation or the observer.

Affect heuristic: basing a decision on an emotional reaction rather than a calculation of risks and benefits.

Ambiguity effect: the avoidance of options for which missing information makes the probability seem "unknown".

Anchoring effect: the tendency to rely too heavily, or "anchor," on a past reference or on one trait or piece of information when making decisions (also called "insufficient adjustment").

Attentional bias: neglect of relevant data when making judgments of a correlation or association.

Attribute substitution: making a complex, difficult judgment by unconsciously substituting an easier judgment.

Authority bias: the tendency to value an ambiguous stimulus (e.g., an art performance) according to the opinion of someone who is seen as an authority on the topic.

Availability cascade: a self-reinforcing process in which a collective belief gains more and more plausibility through its increasing repetition in public discourse (or "repeat something long enough and it will become true").

Availability heuristic: estimating what is more likely by what is more available in memory, which is biased toward vivid, unusual, or emotionally charged examples.

Bandwagon effect: the tendency to do (or believe) things because many other people do (or believe) the same. Related to groupthink and herd behavior.

Base rate fallacy: ignoring available statistical data in favor of particulars.

Belief bias: an effect where someone's evaluation of the logical strength of an argument is biased by the believability of the conclusion.

Bias blind spot: the tendency not to compensate for one's own cognitive biases.

Capability bias: The tendency to believe that the closer average performance is to a target, the tighter the distribution of the data set.

Choice-supportive bias: the tendency to remember one's choices as better than they actually were.

Clustering illusion: the tendency to see patterns where actually none exist.

Confirmation bias: the tendency to search for or interpret information in a way that confirms one's preconceptions.

Congruence bias: the tendency to test hypotheses exclusively through direct testing, in contrast to tests of possible alternative hypotheses.

Conjunction fallacy: the tendency to assume that specific conditions are more probable than general ones.

Consistency bias: incorrectly remembering one's past attitudes and behavior as resembling present attitudes and behavior.

Contrast effect: the enhancement or diminishing of a weight or other measurement when compared with a recently observed contrasting object.

Cryptomnesia: a form of misattribution where a memory is mistaken for imagination.

Déformation professionnelle: the tendency to look at things according to the conventions of one's own profession, forgetting any broader point of view.

Denomination effect: the tendency to spend more money when it is denominated in small amounts (e.g. coins) than large amounts (e.g. bills).

Disposition effect: the tendency to sell assets that have increased in value but hold assets that have decreased in value.

Disregard of regression toward the mean: the tendency to expect extreme performance to continue.

Distinction bias: the tendency to view two options as more dissimilar when evaluating them simultaneously than when evaluating them separately.

Egocentric bias: occurs when people claim more responsibility for themselves for the results of a joint action than an outside observer would.

Egocentric bias: recalling the past in a self-serving manner, e.g. remembering one's exam grades as being better than they were, or remembering a caught fish as being bigger than it was.

Endowment effect: "the fact that people often demand much more to give up an object than they would be willing to pay to acquire it".

Experimenter's or Expectation bias: the tendency for experimenters to believe, certify, and publish data that agree with their expectations for the outcome of an experiment, and to disbelieve, discard, or downgrade the corresponding weightings for data that appear to conflict with those expectations.

Extraordinarity bias: the tendency to value an object more than others in the same category as a result of an extraordinarity of that object that does not, in itself, change the value.

False consensus effect: the tendency for people to overestimate the degree to which others agree with them.

False memory: confusion of imagination with memory, or the confusion of true memories with false memories.

Focusing effect: prediction bias occurring when people place too much importance on one aspect of an event; causes error in accurately predicting the utility of a future outcome.

Forer effect (aka Barnum Effect): the tendency to give high accuracy ratings to descriptions of their personality that supposedly are tailored specifically for them, but are in fact vague and general enough to apply to a wide range of people. For example, horoscopes.

Framing: Using an approach or description of the situation or issue that is too narrow. Also framing effect: drawing different conclusions based on how data is presented.

Fundamental attribution error: the tendency for people to over-emphasize personality-based explanations for behaviors observed in others while under-emphasizing the role and power of situational influences on the same behavior (see also actor-observer bias, group attribution error, positivity effect, and negativity effect).

Gambler's fallacy: the tendency to think that future probabilities are altered by past events, when in reality they are unchanged. Results from an erroneous conceptualization of the Law of large numbers. For example, "I've flipped heads with this coin five times consecutively, so the chance of tails coming out on the sixth flip is much greater than heads." .

Halo effect: the tendency for a person's positive or negative traits to "spill over" from one area of their personality to another in others' perceptions of them (see also physical attractiveness stereotype).

Hawthorne effect: the tendency of people to perform or perceive differently when they know that they are being observed.

Herd instinct: Common tendency to adopt the opinions and follow the behaviors of the majority to feel safer and to avoid conflict.

Hindsight bias: filtering memory of past events through present knowledge, so that those events look more predictable.

Hyperbolic discounting: the tendency for people to have a stronger preference for more immediate payoffs relative to later payoffs, where the tendency increases the closer to the present both payoffs are.

Illusion of asymmetric insight: people perceive their knowledge of their peers to surpass their peers' knowledge of them.

Illusion of control: the tendency for human beings to believe they can control or at least influence outcomes that they clearly cannot.

Illusion of transparency: people overestimate others' ability to know them, and they also overestimate their ability to know others.

Illusory correlation: beliefs that inaccurately suppose a relationship between a certain type of action and an effect.

Illusory superiority: overestimating one's desirable qualities, and underestimating undesirable qualities, relative to other people. Also known as Superiority bias (also known as "Lake Wobegon effect", "better-than-average effect", "superiority bias", or Dunning-Kruger effect).

Impact bias: the tendency for people to overestimate the length or the intensity of the impact of future feeling states.

Information bias: the tendency to seek information even when it cannot affect action.

Ingroup bias: the tendency for people to give preferential treatment to others they perceive to be members of their own groups.

Interloper effect: the tendency to value third party consultation as objective, confirming, and without motive. Also consultation paradox, the conclusion that solutions proposed by existing personnel within an organization are less likely to receive support than from those recruited for that purpose.

Irrational escalation: the tendency to make irrational decisions based upon rational decisions in the past or to justify actions already taken.

Just-world phenomenon: the tendency for people to believe that the world is just and therefore people "get what they deserve." .

Loss aversion: "the disutility of giving up an object is greater than the utility associated with acquiring it". (see also sunk cost effects and Endowment effect).

Ludic fallacy: the analysis of chance-related problems according to the belief that the unstructured randomness found in life resembles the structured randomness found in games, ignoring the non-gaussian distribution of many real-world results.

Mere exposure effect: the tendency for people to express undue liking for things merely because they are familiar with them.

Money illusion: the tendency of people to concentrate on the nominal (face value) of money rather than its value in terms of purchasing power.

Moral credential effect: the tendency of a track record of non-prejudice to increase subsequent prejudice.

Need for Closure: the need to reach a verdict in important matters; to have an answer and to escape the feeling of doubt and uncertainty. The personal context (time or social pressure) might increase this bias.

Negativity bias: phenomenon by which humans pay more attention to and give more weight to negative than positive experiences or other kinds of information.

Neglect of prior base rates effect: the tendency to neglect known odds when reevaluating odds in light of weak evidence.

Neglect of probability: the tendency to completely disregard probability when making a decision under uncertainty.

Normalcy bias: the refusal to plan for, or react to, a disaster which has never happened before.

Not Invented Here: the tendency to ignore that a product or solution already exists, because its source is seen as an "enemy" or as "inferior".

Notational bias: a form of cultural bias in which the notational conventions of recording data biases the appearance of that data toward (or away from) the system upon which the notational schema is based.

Observer-expectancy effect: when a researcher expects a given result and therefore unconsciously manipulates an experiment or misinterprets data in order to find it (see also subject-expectancy effect).

Omission bias: the tendency to judge harmful actions as worse, or less moral, than equally harmful omissions (inactions).

Optimism bias: the systematic tendency to be over-optimistic about the outcome of planned actions.

Ostrich effect: ignoring an obvious (negative) situation.

Outcome bias: the tendency to judge a decision by its eventual outcome instead of based on the quality of the decision at the time it was made.

Outgroup homogeneity bias: individuals see members of their own group as being relatively more varied than members of other groups.

Overconfidence effect: excessive confidence in one's own answers to questions. For example, for certain types of question, answers that people rate as "99% certain" turn out to be wrong 40% of the time.

Pareidolia: a vague and random stimulus (often an image or sound) is perceived as significant, e.g., seeing images of animals or faces in clouds, the man in the moon, and hearing hidden messages on records played in reverse.

Planning fallacy: the tendency to underestimate task-completion times.

Positive outcome bias: a tendency in prediction to overestimate the probability of good things happening to them (see also wishful thinking, optimism bias, and valence effect).

Post-purchase rationalization: the tendency to persuade oneself through rational argument that a purchase was a good value.

Primacy effect: the tendency to weigh initial events more than subsequent events.

Projection bias: the tendency to unconsciously assume that others share the same or similar thoughts, beliefs, values, or positions.

Pseudocertainty effect: the tendency to make risk-averse choices if the expected outcome is positive, but make risk-seeking choices to avoid negative outcomes.

Reactance: the urge to do the opposite of what someone wants you to do out of a need to resist a perceived attempt to constrain your freedom of choice.

Recency effect: the tendency to weigh recent events more than earlier events (see also peak-end rule).

Reminiscence bump: the effect that people tend to recall more personal events from adolescence and early adulthood than from other lifetime periods.

Representativeness heuristic: judging probabilities on the basis of resemblance.

Restraint bias: the tendency to overestimate one's ability to show restraint in the face of temptation.

Rosy retrospection: the tendency to rate past events more positively than they had actually rated them when the event occurred.

Selection bias: a distortion of evidence or data that arises from the way that the data are collected.

Selective perception: the tendency for expectations to affect perception.

Self-fulfilling prophecy: the tendency to engage in behaviors that elicit results which will (consciously or not) confirm existing attitudes.

Self-serving bias (also called "behavioral confirmation effect"): the tendency to claim more responsibility for successes than failures. It may also manifest itself as a tendency for people to evaluate ambiguous information in a way beneficial to their interests (see also group-serving bias).

Self-serving bias: perceiving oneself responsible for desirable outcomes but not responsible for undesirable ones.

Semmelweis reflex: the tendency to reject new evidence that contradicts an established paradigm.

Status quo bias: the tendency for people to like things to stay relatively the same (see also loss aversion, endowment effect, and system justification).

Stereotyping: expecting a member of a group to have certain characteristics without having actual information about that individual.

Subadditivity effect: the tendency to judge probability of the whole to be less than the probabilities of the parts.

Subjective validation: perception that something is true if a subject's belief demands it to be true. Also assigns perceived connections between coincidences.

Suggestibility: a form of misattribution where ideas suggested by a questioner are mistaken for memory.

System justification: the tendency to defend and bolster the status quo. Existing social, economic, and political arrangements tend to be preferred, and alternatives disparaged sometimes even at the expense of individual and collective self-interest. (See also status quo bias.) .

Telescoping effect: the effect that recent events appear to have occurred more remotely and remote events appear to have occurred more recently.

Texas sharpshooter fallacy: the fallacy of selecting or adjusting a hypothesis after the data is collected, making it impossible to test the hypothesis fairly. Refers to the concept of firing shots at a barn door, drawing a circle around the best group, and declaring that to be the target.

Trait ascription bias: the tendency for people to view themselves as relatively variable in terms of personality, behavior and mood while viewing others as much more predictable.

Ultimate attribution error: Similar to the fundamental attribution error, in this error a person is likely to make an internal attribution to an entire group instead of the individuals within the group.

Von Restorff effect: the tendency for an item that "stands out like a sore thumb" to be more likely to be remembered than other items.

Well travelled road effect: underestimation of the duration taken to traverse oft-travelled routes and over-estimate the duration taken to traverse less familiar routes.

Wishful thinking: the formation of beliefs and the making of decisions according to what is pleasing to imagine instead of by appeal to evidence or rationality.

Zero-risk bias: preference for reducing a small risk to zero over a greater reduction in a larger risk.

Growth

Discounts	3%	4%	5%	6%	7%	8%	9%	10%	11%	12%	13%	14%	15%	16%	17%	18%	19%	20%
5%	3.53%	4.53%	5.54%	6.55%	7.55%	8.56%	9.56%	10.57%	11.57%	12.58%	13.58%	14.59%	15.59%	16.60%	17.60%	18.61%	19.61%	20.62%
10%	4.09%	5.10%	6.11%	7.12%	8.13%	9.14%	10.15%	11.17%	12.18%	13.19%	14.20%	15.21%	16.22%	17.23%	18.24%	19.25%	20.26%	21.27%
15%	4.69%	5.70%	6.72%	7.74%	8.75%	9.77%	10.79%	11.80%	12.82%	13.84%	14.85%	15.87%	16.88%	17.90%	18.92%	19.93%	20.95%	21.97%
20%	5.32%	6.35%	7.37%	8.39%	9.41%	10.44%	11.46%	12.48%	13.50%	14.53%	15.55%	16.57%	17.59%	18.62%	19.64%	20.66%	21.69%	22.71%
25%	6.01%	7.04%	8.06%	9.09%	10.12%	11.15%	12.18%	13.21%	14.24%	15.27%	16.30%	17.33%	18.36%	19.39%	20.41%	21.44%	22.47%	23.50%
30%	6.74%	7.78%	8.81%	9.85%	10.89%	11.92%	12.96%	13.99%	15.03%	16.07%	17.10%	18.14%	19.18%	20.21%	21.25%	22.28%	23.32%	24.36%
35%	7.53%	8.58%	9.62%	10.67%	11.71%	12.75%	13.80%	14.84%	15.89%	16.93%	17.97%	19.02%	20.06%	21.11%	22.15%	23.19%	24.24%	25.28%
40%	8.40%	9.45%	10.50%	11.56%	12.61%	13.66%	14.71%	15.77%	16.82%	17.87%	18.92%	19.97%	21.03%	22.08%	23.13%	24.18%	25.24%	26.29%
45%	9.35%	10.41%	11.47%	12.53%	13.59%	14.65%	15.72%	16.78%	17.84%	18.90%	19.96%	21.02%	22.08%	23.15%	24.21%	25.27%	26.33%	27.39%
50%	10.39%	11.46%	12.54%	13.61%	14.68%	15.75%	16.82%	17.90%	18.97%	20.04%	21.11%	22.18%	23.25%	24.33%	25.40%	26.47%	27.54%	28.61%
55%	11.56%	12.65%	13.73%	14.81%	15.89%	16.98%	18.06%	19.14%	20.23%	21.31%	22.39%	23.48%	24.56%	25.64%	26.73%	27.81%	28.89%	29.98%
60%	12.88%	13.98%	15.08%	16.17%	17.27%	18.36%	19.46%	20.56%	21.65%	22.75%	23.84%	24.94%	26.04%	27.13%	28.23%	29.32%	30.42%	31.51%
65%	14.40%	15.51%	16.62%	17.73%	18.84%	19.95%	21.07%	22.18%	23.29%	24.40%	25.51%	26.62%	27.73%	28.84%	29.95%	31.06%	32.17%	33.28%
70%	16.18%	17.31%	18.43%	19.56%	20.69%	21.82%	22.95%	24.07%	25.20%	26.33%	27.46%	28.59%	29.71%	30.84%	31.97%	33.10%	34.23%	35.35%
75%	18.32%	19.46%	20.61%	21.76%	22.91%	24.06%	25.21%	26.36%	27.51%	28.65%	29.80%	30.95%	32.10%	33.25%	34.40%	35.55%	36.70%	37.84%
80%	20.99%	22.16%	23.33%	24.51%	25.68%	26.86%	28.03%	29.21%	30.38%	31.56%	32.73%	33.91%	35.08%	36.26%	37.43%	38.61%	39.78%	40.95%
85%	24.52%	25.73%	26.93%	28.14%	29.35%	30.56%	31.77%	32.98%	34.19%	35.40%	36.61%	37.81%	39.02%	40.23%	41.44%	42.65%	43.88%	45.07%
90%	29.67%	30.93%	32.19%	33.45%	34.71%	35.96%	37.22%	38.48%	39.74%	41.00%	42.26%	43.52%	44.78%	46.04%	47.29%	48.55%	49.81%	51.07%

Effective Yield of a Bargain Purchase after 10-years.

(Chart designed by Mr. Bakul Lalla)

This chart is a teaser that is included here to encourage readers to read my first book, "The Four Filters Invention of Warren Buffett and Charlie Munger." The book is available on Amazon.com.

It is also included to encourage careful sensible investing. How can one use the chart in long term investing? Once you have a suitable investment candidate that fulfills the first three filters, estimate the intrinsic value. Then, using your "estimated discount" (intrinsic value minus market price), look to where the discount intersects with a reasonable growth rate to find an estimate for an effective yield for your investment when held for ten years.

How We Can Restore Confidence

The Washington Post

By Charles T. Munger

Wednesday, February 11, 2009

Our situation is dire. Moderate booms and busts are inevitable in free-market capitalism. But a boom-bust cycle as gross as the one that caused our present misery is dangerous, and recurrences should be prevented. The country is understandably depressed -- mired in issues involving fiscal stimulus, which is needed, and improvements in bank strength. A key question: Should we opt for even more pain now to gain a better future? For instance, should we create new controls to stamp out much sin and folly and thus dampen future booms? The answer is yes.

Sensible reform cannot avoid causing significant pain, which is worth enduring to gain extra safety and more exemplary conduct. And only when there is strong public revulsion, such as exists today, can legislators minimize the influence of powerful special interests enough to bring about needed revisions in law.

Many contributors to our over-the-top boom, which led to the gross bust, are known. They include insufficient controls over morality and prudence in banks and investment banks; undesirable conduct among investment banks; greatly expanded financial leverage, aided by direct or implied use of government credit; and extreme excess, sometimes amounting to fraud, in the promotion of consumer credit. Unsound accounting was widespread.

There was also great excess in highly leveraged speculation of all kinds. Perhaps real estate speculation did the most damage. But the new trading in derivative contracts involving corporate bonds took the prize. This system, in which completely unrelated entities bet trillions with virtually no regulation, created two things: a gambling facility that mimicked the 1920s "bucket shops" wherein bookie-customer types could bet on security prices, instead of horse races, with almost no one owning any securities, and, second, a large group of entities that had an intense desire that certain companies should fail. Croupier types pushed this system, assisted by academics who should have known better. Unfortunately, they convinced regulators that denizens of our financial system would use the new speculative opportunities without causing more harm than benefit.

Considering the huge profit potential of these activities, it may seem unlikely that any important opposition to reform would come from parties other than conventional, moneyed special interests. But many in academia, too, will resist. It is important that reform plans mix moral and accounting concepts with traditional economic concepts. Many economists take fierce pride in opposing that sort of mixed reasoning. But what these economists like to think about is functionally intertwined, in complex ways, with what they don't like to think about. Those who resist the wider thinking are acting as engineers would if they rounded pi from 3.14 to an even 3 to simplify their calculations. The result is a kind of willful ignorance that fails to understand much that is important.

Moreover, rationality in the current situation requires even more stretch in economic thinking. Public deliberations should include not only private morality and accounting issues but also issues of public morality, particularly with regard to taxation. The United States has long run large, concurrent trade and fiscal deficits while, to its own great advantage, issuing the main reserve currency of a deeply troubled and deeply interdependent world. That world now faces new risks from an expanding group of nations possessing nuclear weapons. And so the United States may now have a duty similar to the one that, in the danger that followed World War II, caused the Marshall Plan to be approved in a bipartisan consensus and rebuild a devastated Europe.

The consensus was grounded in Secretary of State George Marshall's concept of moral duty, supplemented by prudential considerations. The modern form of this duty would demand at least some increase in conventional taxes or the imposition of some new consumption taxes. In so doing, the needed and cheering economic message, "We will do what it takes," would get a corollary: "and without unacceptably devaluing our money." Surely the more complex message is more responsible, considering that, first, our practices of running twin deficits depend on drawing from reserves of trust that are not infinite and, second, the message of the corollary would not be widely believed unless it was accompanied by some new taxes.

Moreover, increasing taxes in some instances might easily gain bipartisan approval. Surely both political parties can now join in taxing the "carry" part of the compensation of hedge fund managers as if it was more constructively earned in, say, cab driving.

Much has been said and written recently about bipartisanship, and success in a bipartisan approach might provide great advantage here. Indeed, it is conceivable that, if legislation were adopted in a bipartisan way, instead of as a consequence of partisan hatred, the solutions that curbed excess and improved safeguards in our financial system could reduce national pain instead of increasing it. After the failure of so much that was assumed, the public needs a restoration of confidence. And the surest way to gain the confidence of others is to deserve the confidence of others, as Marshall did when he helped cause passage of some of the best legislation ever enacted.

Creating in a bipartisan manner a legislative package that covers many subjects will be difficult. As they work together in the coming weeks, officials might want to consider a precedent that helped establish our republic. The deliberative rules of the Constitutional Convention of 1787 worked wonders in fruitful compromise and eventually produced the U.S. Constitution. With no Marshall figure, trusted by all, amid today's legislators, perhaps the Founding Fathers can once more serve us.

Ten Things I Learned While Trading for Victor Niederhoffer

By James Altucher

http://blogs.wsj.com/financial-adviser/2010/02/25/ten-things-i-learned-while-trading-for-victor-niederhoffer/

I traded for Victor Niederhoffer for about a year starting in 2003. I was up slightly more than 100% for him, primarily trading futures using a quantitative approach. During that period I had one down month: June 2003.

Victor was a top trader for George Soros before starting his own fund in the '90s and then writing the classic investment text "Education of a Speculator." He then suffered one of several blowups in his career when his fund crashed to zero while on the wrong side of a couple of bets during the Asian currency crisis in 1997 (most notably, he was short S&P puts when the market crashed that year).

Despite that, Victor has consistently traded his own portfolio quite successfully and is one of the best traders I've seen in action. He still posts his daily comments on trading and the markets at his site dailyspeculations.com.

Here are 10 things I learned during my time trading for Victor:

1.) Test, test, test. Test everything you can. If someone says to me, "There's inflation coming so you better short stocks," I know right away the person doesn't test and will lose money. Data is available for almost anything you can imagine. (In my talks, I always discuss the "blizzard system" based on data of what the stock market does depending on how many inches of snow have fallen in Central Park that day). Victor and his crew would spend all day testing ideas: What historically happens to the market on a Fed day? What happens on options expiration day if the two prior days were negative? Do stocks that start with the letter "x" outperform? Nothing was beyond testing.

2.) Optimism. There's plenty of reasons every day to assume the world is going to end. The media is constantly speculating about imminent financial collapse, hyperinflation, peak oil, pandemics, terrorism, etc. One of Victor's favorite books, which I highly recommend, is "Triumph of the Optimists," which shows the success of the U.S. markets over the past century over other markets and asset classes. Yes, the markets take a hit. But invariably buying dips (and being careful not to get wiped out) will be a long-term strategy for success.

3.) Fearlessness. I had a big March 2003 trading for Victor. The market was threatening to go to new lows at the advent of the Iraqi war. I went long and strong and had a great month. Then, for the rest of the year, for fear of destroying a great track record, I would go up a few percentage points at the beginning of each month and then coast for the rest of the month, probably leaving another 100% or so on the table as I passed on trading many high probability situations. I always suspected Victor was very disappointed in me for that. When you have a high probability situation, trade it and trade it big.

4.) Everything Is Connected. Whether you are studying baseball, checkers, trees, wars – all contain patterns similar to the patterns we see every day in trading. Sometimes the best way to get perspective on your trading is to study something seemingly unrelated and to then consider the analogies.

5.) Ayn Rand. There's a lot of retrospectives right now about Rand, one of Victor's favorite authors. I don't care much for the so-called Objectivism or Rand's views on capitalism, but what struck me about her books was the emphasis on competence. Her novels are about competence and the personal gratification one gets by being good at what you do, whether it's building railroads, designing a building, trading or cleaning a house.

6.) Warren Buffett. Victor is not a fan of Warren Buffett. This forced me to look at Buffett in a whole new way. Is Buffett a value investor? What other tricks of the trade has Buffett used over the years? I ended up reading every biography of Buffett, going through four decades of SEC filings, and pouring over not only his Berkshire letters but his prior letters from his hedge fund days (1957-1969). The result was my book, "Trade Like Warren Buffett."

7.) The First Day of the Month. It's probably the most important trading day of the month, as inflows come in from 401(k) plans, IRAs, etc. and mutual fund have to go out there and put this new money into stocks. Over the past 16 years, buying the close on SPY (the S&P 500 ETF) on the last day of the month and selling one day later would result in a successful trade 63% of the time with an average return of 0.37% (as opposed to 0.03% and a 50%-50% success rate if you buy any random day during this period). Various conditions take place that improve this result significantly. For instance, one time I was visiting Victor's office on the first day of a month and one of his traders showed me a system and said, "If you show this to anyone we will have to kill you." Basically, the system was: If the last half of the last day of the month was negative and the first half of the first day of the month was negative, buy at 11 a.m. and hold for the rest of the day. "This is an ATM machine" the trader told me. I leave it to the reader to test this system.

8.) Always Protect the Downside. This is learned by negative example. As Nassim Taleb has pointed out ad nauseum, Black Swans occur. (See the Malcolm Gladwell article on Taleb to see Taleb's thoughts on Victor.) No matter how much you test, there will be a "this time is different" moment that will force your bank account into oblivion. I trade a strategy based on selling puts and calls at levels where my software thinks its statistically unlikely the market hits those levels before the next options expirations day. But I also use some of the premium I earned from selling those puts and calls to buy slightly further out puts and calls as insurance the market doesn't run away from me. No matter how confident the software is, always protect.

9.) Keep Life Interesting. Victor surrounds himself by games and the people who enjoy them. When I knew him, he took regular checkers lessons, played tennis every day, and has some of the oddest collections I've ever seen. He stands out on a crowded city street and seems to spend part of each day seeking out new and interesting experiences. He often asked me what I'd been reading and if it was trading related he was disappointed. Trading is ultimately a window into the psyche of the world at that moment. Uncovering the nuances of that psyche is ultimately more important than doing the latest test on what happens after a Fed announcement (but, on that point, tests have shown that whatever the market is doing before a 2:15p.m. Fed announcement on Fed days, chances are it will reverse after 2:15).

10.) Be Open to New Ideas. In 2002, I was still reeling from the dot-com collapse. I had sold a company near the height of the insanity in 1998 and also started a VC fund that opened up doors in March, 2000, the absolute peak of the market. I was trying to figure out new things to do. I came up with a list of about 30 people I looked up to and came up with 10 ideas for each person about how they could improve their business. To Victor, I sent a series of trading ideas that I had both backtested and had traded successfully. To Jim Cramer, I sent a list of 10 ideas for articles he should write. Of the 30 people, they were the only two who responded and ultimately I ended up managing a little bit of money for Victor and writing for Jim Cramer's site, thestreet.com. I'm grateful for the opportunities that both people created for me.

James Altucher is a managing partner of Formula Capital, an alternative asset management firm, and an author on investment strategies. Unlike Dow Jones reporters, he may have positions in the stocks he writes about.

Factors that can affect the US Dollar.

From the World Economic Forum

Risk Interconnection Map

http://www.weforum.org/documents/riskbrowser2010/risks/#

Intelligent Speculation Framing Worksheet

1. **Economic Understanding of the Speculation:**

2. **Advantages / Disadvantages.**

    A. Advantages:

    B. Disadvantages:

3. **People Involved:**

4. **Price and Value of the Speculation:**

5. **Catalysts and Conditions:**

Notes

Some Thoughts about Bill Ruane
By Paul Lountzis

As I began evaluating job opportunities with value oriented money managers a west coast value investor who was friendly with Bob Goldfarb suggested that given my investment philosophy and approach that I should call Bob at Ruane, Cunniff & Goldfarb. I met with Bob as well as some of the other members of the firm and was asked to return a week later to meet Bill Ruane.

I had followed the firm over the years, primarily through the Sequoia Fund Letters and was both excited and nervous to meet Bill Ruane, one of the best investors in the country. Bill's soft touch was evident the moment I met him and he immediately made me feel comfortable as I visited with him in his office. On his desk were 2 large reports on companies which I had done work on and which the firm owned in the Sequoia Fund. I was eagerly prepared to discuss my investment research at length, hoping that Bill would hire me.

However, Bill's primary focus throughout the interview had nothing to do with my investment research, or hiring me, but rather the health of our newborn son Tyler. Tyler was born in Greenwich Hospital and was diagnosed with an atrial-septal defect - a hole in the upper chambers of his heart. Congenital heart defects are prevalent in about 1 in 115 newborns and

Tyler's specific defect would require surgery which is typically performed when the child is older and stronger with fewer risks at 3 or 4 years of age before they begin school. Tyler, however, had a moderate size hole and would need open heart surgery much sooner. Bill asked numerous questions about Tyler's diagnosis, prognosis, surgeon, hospital, etc. and then asked how much an open heart operation on an infant would cost. Before I could even respond Bill said, "Whatever Tyler's heart surgery costs I/the firm will pay for everything".

Needless to say, I was quite flabbergasted and surprised to be at a job interview, spending the great majority of the interview with one of the country's best investors whose singular focus was on our family and in particular on my son's open heart surgery.

My job interview with Bill Ruane remains one of the most important meetings in my life as I had the opportunity to meet an extraordinary man whose core values, integrity and character were fully evident by his incredibly thoughtful actions. Bill was far more than a terrific investor, which I was already aware of. What I did not know was the truly exceptional human being Bill was and as I often say-Bill was a great investor but an even greater human being. From that moment on his example is one I have tried to emulate and while investing remains an important part of my life being a terrific human being by serving others is far more important.

I might add in closing that Bill and the firm did pay for everything regarding Tyler's open heart surgery-one would expect no less-Bill lived by his word. It is also a pleasure to report that Tyler's surgery at the tender age of 10 months was a complete success. Tyler is now approaching his 20th birthday and is currently in the United States Army serving in Korea.

Few outside of the investment world knew Bill Ruane, (that is how he liked it) and even among those within the investment world who knew of Bill a very small minority knew him well enough to know what a truly extraordinary human being he was. Bill passed away in October 2005 and while the world lost a great investor it lost an even greater person. Our family is so grateful that he touched our lives in such a special way and we know he is still cheering Tyler on.

ENDNOTES

[1] Charlie Munger talk at Harvard Law School, 2001.

[2] Benjamin Graham Lecture Number Ten. These lectures are from the series entitled Current Problems in Security Analysis that Mr. Graham presented at the New York Institute of Finance from September 1946 to February 1947. The book provides an abridged version of this content. The full text of the transcripts are contained within this website.
http://www.wiley.com/legacy/products/subject/finance/bgraham/benlec4.html
The Rediscovered Benjamin Graham: Selected Writings of the Wall Street Legend, by Janet Lowe.

[3] The Four Filters, Berkshire Chairman's Letter to Shareholders, 2007.

[4] Berkshire Hathaway Annual Meeting, 2004.

[5] Benjamin Graham Lecture Number Ten. These lectures are from the series entitled Current Problems in Security Analysis that Mr. Graham presented at the New York Institute of Finance from September 1946 to February 1947.

[6] Berkshire Hathaway Annual Meeting, 1995.

[7] (The Psychology of Human Misjudgment Revised Speech by Charles T. Munger), Kaufman, Peter D., Poor Charlie's Almanack, Virginia Beach, VA: PCA Publication, LLC, 2005.

[8] The Four Filters, Berkshire Chairman's Letter to Shareholders, 2007.

[9] A Lesson on Elementary, Worldly Wisdom As It Relates To Investment Management & Business". Charles Munger, USC Business School, 1994.

[10] Buffett Partnership Letter, 1961.

[11] Berkshire Chairman's Letter to Shareholders, 1997.

[12] Loss Development Methods For Association of Insurance Compliance Professionals (Of the Midwest), presentation by Jim Shoenfelt, ACAS. Found via Google Search.

[13] Practical Speculation. Victor Niederhoffer and Laurel Kenner. Wiley. February, 2003.

[14] Takemura, K. (1992) Effect of decision time on framing of decision: A case of risky choice. behavior. Psychologia, 35, 180-185.
Takemura, K. (1994). Influence of elaboration on the framing of decisions. Journal of Psychology, 128, 33–39.

[15] Berkshire Chairman's Letter to Shareholders,

1999,(www.berkshirehathaway.com/1999ar/1999final.html)

[16] Charlie Munger: USC Business School, 1994 Speech: A Lesson on Elementary, Worldly

Wisdom As It Relates To Investment Management & Business.

[17] Charlie Munger: USC Business School, 1994 Speech: A Lesson on Elementary, Worldly
Wisdom As It Relates To Investment Management & Business.

[18] Buffett Partnership Letter, 1960.

[19] Berkshire Chairman's Letter to Shareholders, 1993.

[20] Charles T. Munger quote.

[21] Charlie Munger: USC Business School, 1994 Speech: A Lesson on Elementary, Worldly
Wisdom As It Relates To Investment Management & Business.

[22] Berkshire Hathaway Annual Meeting, 2003.

[23] Warren Buffett, "The Superinvestors of Graham-and-Doddsville," Hermes (Fall 1984).

[24] Berkshire Chairman's Letter to Shareholders, 1993.

[25] Berkshire Chairman's Letter to Shareholders, 2001.

[26] Benjamin Graham Lecture Number Ten. These lectures are from the series entitled Current
Problems in Security Analysis that Mr. Graham presented at the New York Institute of Finance
from September 1946 to February 1947.

[27] FORBES(1974), Warren Buffett Interview, 1974.

[28] Berkshire Chairman's Letter to Shareholders, 1992.

[29] Berkshire Chairman's Letter to Shareholders, 1981.
[30] Berkshire Chairman's Letter to Shareholders, 1988.

[31] Porter, Michael E., Competitive Advantage: Creating and Sustaining Superior Performance.
Free Press, 1998.

[32]Steinhardt, Michael., autobiography: "No Bull: My Life in and out of Markets. Hoboken NJ:
John Wiley & Sons, 2001

[33] Warren Buffett, "The Superinvestors of Graham-and-Doddsville," Hermes (Fall 1984).

[34] A term used by successful Wall Street Trader, Michael Steinhardt.

[35] From a talk given at the University of Florida, quoted in the Miami Herald (December 27, 1998), quoted in Kilpatrick, Of Permanent Value (2004), 1350.

[36] Berkshire Chairman's Letter to Shareholders, 1980.
[37] Berkshire Chairman's Letter to Shareholders, 1989.
[38] Berkshire Chairman's Letter to Shareholders, 1981.
[39] Berkshire Chairman's Letter to Shareholders, 1982.
[40] Berkshire Chairman's Letter to Shareholders, 1993.

[41] Charles Mizrahi, "Getting Started in Value Investing", Hoboken NJ: John Wiley & Sons, 2006

[42] Berkshire Chairman's Letter to Shareholders, 1990.

[43] Greenwald, Bruce and Kahn, Judd, Competition Demystified, New York NY: Penguin Group, 2005

[44] Michael E. Porter, Competitive Advantage: Creating and Sustaining Superior Performance (New York: The Free Press, 1985) p. 73.

[45] "Able and honest people", Berkshire Chairman's Letter to Shareholders, 2002.

[46] Research looks at why people gamble. Dr. Dave Clarke, School of Psychology at New Zealand's Massey University http://www.news-medical.net/news/2004/06/14/2416.aspx June, 2004.

[47] Berkshire Hathaway Owner's Manual, www.berkshirehathaway.com/owners.html

[48] Berkshire Chairman's Letter to Shareholders, 1994.

[49] Robert Miles, The Warren Buffett CEO (Hoboken, NJ: Wiley, 2003).

[50] Berkshire Chairman's Letter to Shareholders, 1992.

[51] Berkshire Chairman's Letter to Shareholders, 2000.

[52] The Theory of Reflexivity. Speech by George Soros, The MIT Department of Economics World Economy Laboratory Conference Washington, D.C. Delivered April 26, 1994.

[53] Chapter 14. Mergers and Acquisitions. Deal Heat and Other Deadly Sins. Winning. By Jack Welch and Suzy Welch. Harper Business. 2005.

[54] John Burr Williams, The Theory of Investment Value (Cambridge: Harvard University Press, 1938), pp. 186-91.

[55] Benjamin Graham Lecture Number Four, These lectures are from the series entitled Current Problems in Security Analysis that Mr. Graham presented at the New York Institute of Finance from September 1946 to February 1947. The book provides an abridged version of this content. The full text of the transcripts are contained within this website.
http://www.wiley.com/legacy/products/subject/finance/bgraham/benlec4.html
The Rediscovered Benjamin Graham: Selected Writings of the Wall Street Legend, by Janet Lowe.

[56] Berkshire Chairman's Letter to Shareholders, 1992.

[57] Berkshire Chairman's Letter to Shareholders, 1992.

[58] Benjamin Graham Lecture Number Four, These lectures are from the series entitled Current Problems in Security Analysis that Mr. Graham presented at the New York Institute of Finance from September 1946 to February 1947.

[59] John Burr Williams, The Theory of Investment Value (Cambridge: Harvard University Press, 1938), pp. 186-91.

[60] Berkshire Chairman's Letter to Shareholders, 1992.

[61] Berkshire Chairman's Letter to Shareholders, 1992.

[62] Given this uncertainty, it's critical to buy stocks only when their valuation is so low that there's a huge "margin of safety," to use Ben Graham's famous saying. Consider this exchange from the 1996 Berkshire Hathaway (NYSE: BRK.A) annual meeting: "Warren talks about these discounted cash flows," said Vice Chairman Charlie Munger. "I've never seen him do one." "It's true," replied Buffett. "If [a company's value] doesn't just scream out at you, it's too close." A Valuation Rule of Thumb, article by Whitney Tilson (http://www.fool.com/news/foth/2001/foth010731.htm)

[63] Berkshire Chairman's Letter to Shareholders, 2008.

[64] The Greatest Trade Ever: The Behind-the-Scenes Story of How John Paulson Defied Wall Street and Made Financial History by Gregory Zuckerman. Broadway Business, 2009.

[65] The Snowball: Warren Buffett and the Business of Life by Alice Schroeder, Bantam, 2008.

[66] Charlie Munger talk at Harvard Law School, 2001.

[67] When Genius Failed. The Rise and Fall of Long-Term Capital Management. by Roger Lowenstein. Random House Inc. 2001.

[68] The Greatest Trade Ever. The Behind-The-Scenes Story of How John Paulson Defied Wall Street and Made Financial History, Gregory Zuckerman, Broadway Business, 2009.

[69] The Greatest Trade Ever. Book Review. By Daniel Gross | Newsweek Web Exclusive. http://www.newsweek.com/id/221924 Nov 10, 2009.

[70] Charlie Munger talk at Harvard Law School, 2001.

[71] Charlie Munger talk at Harvard Law School, 2001.

Printed in Great Britain by
Amazon.co.uk, Ltd.,
Marston Gate.